Austria
Landscape, Art and Culture

AUSTRIA

Landscape, Art and Culture

Texts by Pia Maria Plechl, György Sebestyén,
Johannes Koren, Friedrich Ch. Zauner,
Humbert Fink, Rudolf Bayr, Franz Caramelle,
Walter Lingenhöle
Photographs by Hella Pflanzer

Pinguin-Verlag, Innsbruck

Photographic sources:
Hans Bohaumilitzky 113, 114a, 118/119; Lichtbildstelle des Bundesministeriums
für Land- und Forstwirtschaft 25c; Marita Janka 96; Löbl-Schreyer 32b;
Erik Pflanzer 75, 132a, 133c; Herbert Pirker 48, 49, 50c, 50d, 51, 54/55, 58/59,
60, 77b, 78a, 78c, 80, 153b; Kurt Roth 90/91, 150/151, 152; all other
photographs by Hella Pflanzer.

English translation: Jacqueline Schweighofer

Edition 1998

© Copyright 1993 by Pinguin-Verlag,
A-6021 Innsbruck
All rights reserved
Printing and binding: Druckerei Theiss GmbH, A-9400 Wolfsberg
Colour reproductions: Tiroler Repro, A-6020 Innsbruck
Typesetting: Lasersatz Maringer, A-5751 Maishofen
Printed in Austria
ISBN 3-7016-2412-7

CONTENTS

FOREWORD 7
Federal President Dr. Thomas Klestil

CHRONOLOGY
OF AUSTRIA'S
HISTORY 9

VIENNA 15
Pia Maria Plechl

LOWER AUSTRIA 39
Pia Maria Plechl

BURGENLAND 65
György Sebestyén

STYRIA 85
Johannes Koren

UPPER AUSTRIA 105
Friedrich Ch. Zauner

CARINTHIA 125
Humbert Fink

SALZBURG 145
Rudolf Bayr

TYROL 165
Franz Caramelle

VORARLBERG 185
Walter Lingenhöle

The Federal President

Magnificent scenery and marvellous cultural works constitute Austria's greatest treasures. Thus it is not merely by chance that our homeland still remains one of Europe's most popular travel and holiday destinations.

Between the Pannonian atmosphere of the Neusiedler See in the east and Lake Constance, set between the Alps and the Bregenzerwald in the west, the nine Austrian federal provinces cater for practically all tastes with their wealth of landscapes and climatic zones. This applies at least in equal measure to Austria's art and history which are documented in lavish variety in churches and monuments, in castles and costumes, in immortal melodies and in profound words.

This book has successfully captured many facets of the Austrian regions, imparting them in such a way that the reader can either recognize himself therein or is prompted to visit this or that province, to view cultural monuments, to take part in festivities, to perceive and to experience at first hand the knowledge, the convictions and the mentality inherent in our traditions.

At a time when Europe is drawing closer together Austria can and must play its established part as a catalyst in the heart of this continent. The auspices are favourable: the political barriers have fallen, a strong sense of solidarity is forming, albeit painfully, among the states and the peoples. Vision and dynamic creativity is required in order to step into the future with awareness. Austria can and will make a decisive contribution because it is superbly equipped to do so.

Accordingly I trust that this book will be well received; I wish its readers true enjoyment and our country many new friends.

Chronology of Austria's History

BC	Initial Neolithic settlements (statuette of Venus excavated at Willendorf in the Wachau area) give rise in the Bronze Age to sizable towns centred around copper deposits.
800—400 BC	Salt mining in the early Iron Age. The "Hallstatt culture" (extensive burial grounds excavated in the Salzkammergut). At the end of the fifth century BC the Celts take possession of the Eastern Alps. Mining flourishes, becoming the basis of large towns (Brigantium-Bregenz) and the kingdom of Noricum.
113—102 BC	The first encounter on Austrian soil between Germanic tribes and the Romans.
15 BC	Drusus establishes the Roman province of Rhaetia (Vorarlberg and Tyrol, Bavaria as far as the Danube). Noricum (Carinthia, Styria, Salzburg, Upper and Lower Austria) subsequently becomes a Roman province.
AD 1—500	Under the Romans the eastern part of Austria forms part of the province of Pannonia. Construction of a road network, promulgation of an administrative code with regulations for the cultivation of vineyards. St. Florian is put to death at Lauriacum-Lorch in the course of Diocletian's persecutions of the Christians. Upon Constantine's proclaiming toleration of Christianity in 313 the first bishoprics on Austrian soil are established at Aguntum (Lienz), Teurnia (Spittal an der Drau) and Virunum (on the Zollfeld). Incursions by Huns in the mid-fifth century and subsequent raids by Germanic tribes herald mass migration. The provinces on Austrian territory separate from the Roman Empire.
500—700	Encroachments by Bavarians from the west and by Slavs and Avars from the east.
700—788	Foundation of the Benedictine abbey of St. Peter in Salzburg by St. Rupert; 739 Salzburg elevated to an independent bishopric by St. Boniface. Christianization with the support of the Dukes of Bavaria. Monastery foundations (Mondsee, Mattsee, Kremsmünster).
788	Bavaria and the march of Carantania (Carinthia) incorporated in the Frankish kingdom.
791—799	Conquest of the Avars by Charlemagne. Foundation of the Carolingian Eastern Mark between Enns, Raab and Drava. Salzburg becomes an archbishopric under Bishop Arno.
881—907	First clashes with the Hungarians. Disintegration of Charlemagne's Eastern Mark.
c. 970	Restoration of the Eastern Mark after the victory at the Lechfeld (955).
976	Margravate awarded to Leopold of Babenberg. Carantania separated from Bavaria and made an independent duchy.
1000—1100	The Babenbergs expand eastwards, founding monasteries (Melk). Salzburg also founds monasteries.
1077—1181	The fortresses of Hohensalzburg and Hohenwerfen are commissioned by the archbishops of Salzburg.
c. 1137	Vienna becomes the Babenberg residence.
1156	Emperor Frederick Barbarossa makes Austria a hereditary duchy and separates it from Bavaria.
1180	Styria becomes a duchy under Ottokar IV of Traungau.
1192	The heritage passes to Leopold V of Babenberg.
1198—1230	Famous poets and minnesingers (Der Kürnberger, Reinmar der Alte, Walther von der Vogelweide) at the court of Leopold VI. Zenith of the Babenberg era.
1246	Frederick II the Quarrelsome, the last Babenberg duke, falls in a battle with the Hungarians at the Leitha.
1278	Rudolf of Habsburg defeats Ottokar II of Bohemia on the Marchfeld.
1282	Rudolf invests his son with possession of Austria and Styria.
1286	Meinhard of Gorizia-Tyrol acquires the duchy of Carinthia.
1314	Friedrich der Schöne of Habsburg and Ludwig of Bavaria simultaneously elected German King. After Friedrich's defeat and imprisonment he renounces the kingship.
1335	Duke Albrecht II acquires Carinthia and Carniola for the Habsburgs.

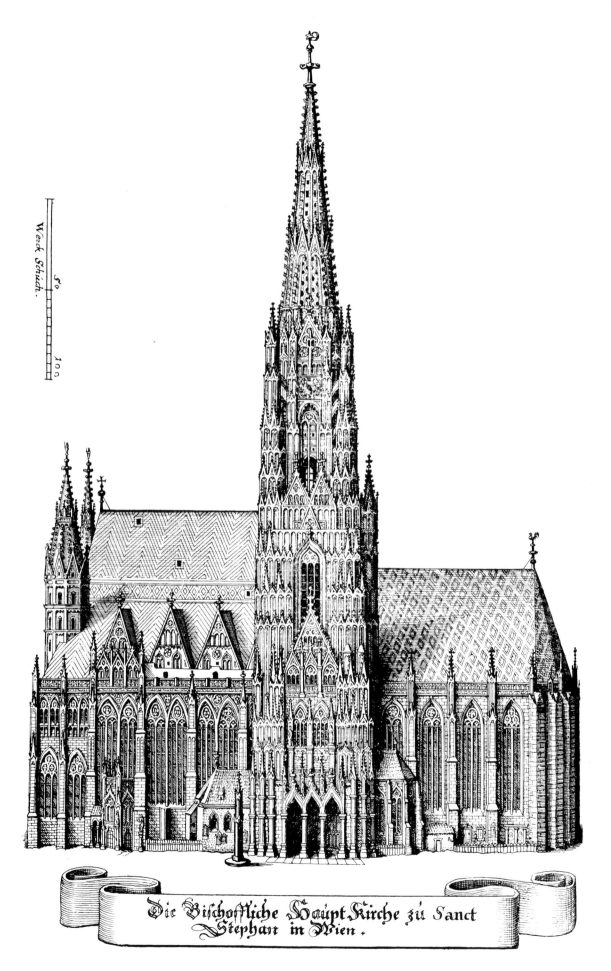

Vienna, St. Stephen's
Cathedral, copper engrav-
ing by Matthäus Merian,
Topographia Austriae
1649.

Weck Schuech.

50

100

Die Bischoffliche Haupt Kirche zu Sanct
Stephan in Wien.

1363	After the death of her son Margarethe Maultasch consigns the Tyrol to Rudolf the Founder.
1365	Foundation of the University of Vienna. Building work on St. Stephen's Cathedral.
1379	The Habsburg domains are divided up between the brothers, Albrecht and Leopold.
1375—1390	The Habsburgs acquire territories in the Bregenzerwald and the County of Feldkirch.
1382	Leopold III acquires Trieste.
1386	Defeat and death of Leopold III at Sempach. Loss of Swiss territories.
1411	Partition agreement between Ernst der Eiserne (Styria) and Friedrich IV (Tyrol).
1437/1438	Albrecht V becomes King of Bohemia, King of Hungary and, as the first Habsburg for over a century, Römischer König.
1439—1493	The long rule of Friedrich V is marked by discord and by Turkish invasions.
1493	Maximilian I rules over the united Habsburg domains and is elected German King.
1496	Marriage of Philip the Handsome to Joanna of Castile-Aragon. Spain and the American colonies under Habsburg rule.
1499	Treaty of Basle. Habsburgs forfeit Switzerland.
1500	Maximilian acquires the County of Gorizia.
1513	Maximilian defeats the French at Guinegate.
1515	Austria acquires the succession to Bohemia and Hungary.
1519	Death of Maximilian I; his grandson, Charles V, inherits a kingdom "upon which the sun never set".
1521/1522	The Habsburgs are divided into an Austrian and a Spanish line.
From c. 1520	Spread of Protestantism in Austria.
1525	Peasant Revolts in Salzburg, the Tyrol and Styria.
1526	Austria acquires Bohemia and Hungary on the death of the Jagiellon king.
1529	First siege of Vienna by the Turks.
1532	Further Turkish raids in Burgenland and Styria.
1556	Upon Charles V's abdication, Ferdinand I becomes Emperor.
1564	Maximilian II succeeds as Emperor. Partition of the domains.
1576	Death of Maximilian and accession of Rudolf II.
1605	Start of the quarrel with Archduke Matthias, Rudolf's brother.
1611	Deposition of Rudolf II.
1612—1619	Already King of Hungary and ruler in Moravia and Austria, Matthias now reigns as Emperor.
1618	Defenestration of Prague, immediate cause of the Thirty Years War.
1619	Ferdinand II succeeds to the imperial crown. Counter-Reformation throughout his domains.
1620	Ferdinand's sovereignty in Bohemia secured after the battle of the White Mountain.
1625	Wallenstein becomes supreme imperial commander.
1634	Deposition and murder of Wallenstein.
1637	Ferdinand III succeeds his father.
1648	The Treaty of Westphalia concludes the Thirty Years War.
1657—1705	Rule of Leopold I who finally unifies the Tyrol with Austria.
1663/1664	Turkish War. Montecucculi's victory at Mogersdorf.
1683	Vienna besieged by the Turks and relieved with the aid of Sobieski. Prince Eugene of Savoy in imperial service.
1697	Prince Eugene's victory over the Turks at Zenta.
1701—1714	War of the Spanish Succession.
1705—1711	Rule of Emperor Joseph I. Prince Eugene's victory in the War of the Spanish Succession. "Charles III" enters Madrid.
1711	Charles reigns the Austrian domains as Charles VI and becomes Emperor.
1713	Pragmatic Sanction secures indivisibility of the monarchy and succession to the throne by a woman.
1714	Treaty of Rastatt. Spain falls to the Bourbons, the Habsburgs receiving Milan, Naples, Sardinia and the Spanish Netherlands.
1736	Marriage of Maria Theresa, Charles VI's daughter, to Francis of Lorraine.
1740	Death of Charles VI. Maria Theresa rules the Habsburg domains.
1740—1763	Maria Theresa defends her claims against Bavaria, Saxony, Prussia and France in the War of the Austrian Succession and the Seven Years War.

1765	Joseph II crowned Emperor after death of Francis I.
1760—1780	Cultural heyday in Austria. Completion of Schönbrunn Palace and the Innsbruck residence.
1780	Death of Maria Theresa.
1780—1790	Joseph II's reforms: abolition of serfdom, religious toleration, reduction of the power of the Church.
1790—1792	Leopold II becomes Emperor. Heyday of Vienna classic (Mozart, Haydn, Beethoven).
1792	Accession of Franz II. Outbreak of First Coalition War with France.
1797	Loss of the Netherlands and Lombardy, acquisition of Venetia, parts of Istria and Dalmatia.
1805	After the Third Coalition War Austria relinquishes Venice to the Kingdom of Italy and the Tyrol and Vorarlberg to Bavaria, acquiring Salzburg.
1806	Franz II resigns the German imperial crown, only remaining Emperor of Austria.
1809	Austria at war with Napoleon, war of liberation in the Tyrol. Archduke Charles defeats Napoleon at Aspern.
1810	Andreas Hofer executed at Mantua. Franz II's daughter, Marie Louise, is married to Napoleon.
1813	Napoleon defeated by Austria, Russia and Prussia at the Battle of Leipzig.
1814—1815	Europe redefined at the Congress of Vienna. Restoration of all Austrian territory. Metternich becomes Europe's leading statesman.
1815—1848	High standard of Biedermeier culture in Austria: Beethoven and Schubert in music; Grillparzer, Stifter, Raimund and Nestroy in literature and theatre; Waldmüller, Schwind, Rudolf von Alt and Daffinger, the painters.
1835	Death of Emperor Franz I; his son, Ferdinand I, accedes to the throne, but state business is carried out by a council of regency.
1839	Opening of the first railway line in Austria.
1848	The March revolution leads to Metternich's fall and the abdication of Ferdinand I.
1848—1916	Reign of Emperor Franz Josef I, the longest rule of any Habsburg in Austria.
1859	War with Sardinia and Napoleon III. Austria has to cede Lombardy.
1866	War with Prussia and Italy results in the loss of Venetia and in Austria's exclusion from Germany.
1867	Settlement with Hungary. Constitution of the dual monarchy.
1878	Austria-Hungary is empowered to occupy Bosnia and Herzegovina at the Congress of Berlin.
1889	Suicide of Crown Prince Rudolph in Mayerling.
c. 1895—1914	Art nouveau. Modernism in literature and music.
1908	Annexation of Bosnia and Herzegovina.
1914	Assassination of Archduke Franz Ferdinand, the heir to the throne, in Sarajevo. Outbreak of the First World War.
1916	Franz Josef's death and accession of Karl I.
1918	Cease-fire. Karl I renounces all share in government. Proclamation of the Republic of Austria with Dr. Karl Renner as its first Chancellor.
1919	Treaty of St. Germain. Austria cedes the South Tyrol, Trieste and Istria to Italy and parts of Carinthia and Styria to Yugoslavia.
1919—1920	Hungary cedes Burgenland to Austria in the Treaty of Trianon.
1922	The Christian Socialists take over from the Social Democrats. Rigorous measures by Dr. Ignaz Seipel, the new Chancellor, to combat inflation.
1924	Introduction of the schilling as currency.
1927	Mass demonstration. The Palace of Justice is set on fire.
1932—1935	Economic crisis after the collapse of the Österreichische Creditanstalt in May 1931. The situation is aggravated by the worldwide Depression.
1932	Dr. Engelbert Dollfuss becomes Chancellor.
1933	Dissolution of the Nationalrat.
1934	Murder of Dollfuss. Dr. Kurt Schuschnigg becomes Chancellor.
1936	Austro-German agreement between Dr. Schuschnigg and Hitler in Berchtesgaden. Mounting National Socialist activities in Austria.

1938	German forces march into Austria. Hitler proclaims Austria's annexation by Germany. Austria becomes the "Ostmark".
1939—1945	Second World War. Air raids. The Red Army in Lower Austria, Burgenland and Styria.
1945	Formation of a provisional Austrian government under Dr. Karl Renner in Russian-occupied Vienna. After Germany's capitulation in May Austria is divided into four zones, occupied by the USA, Great Britain, France and the Soviet Union.
1955	After lengthy negotiations the Austrian State Treaty is signed in Vienna. The occupation forces leave Austria. Reopening of the State Opera House in Vienna.
1964	Winter Olympic Games in Innsbruck.
1966	After two decades of coalition the Austrian People's Party form a Government.
1970	Election of the Socialists with Dr. Bruno Kreisky as Chancellor.
1980	Celebrations to mark the 25th anniversary of the State Treaty. Dr. Rudolf Kirchschläger is elected Federal President for a second term.
1981	Heavy losses by Austrian banks in the biggest collapse of companies since 1945.
1982	Alpine World Skiing Championships in Schladming.
1983	The SPÖ loses its absolute majority in the general election. The FPÖ becomes minor coalition partner.
	Seefeld is chosen as the venue for the Nordic Skiing Championships.
1985	Seefeld hosts the Nordic Skiing World Championships.
1986	Dr. Kurt Waldheim is elected Federal President.
	Dr. Jörg Haider becomes the leader of the FPÖ. After the general election a fourth party, the Green Alternative List, enters the National Assembly.
1987	The SPÖ and the ÖVP form a grand coalition.
	Dr. Vranitzky replaces Dr. Sinowatz as Chancellor, both parties refuse to cooperate with Haider's FPÖ.
1987 to 1991	The federal parliamentary elections in nine provinces show a trend away from absolute majorities.
1989	In the name of the Federal Government Dr. Alois Mock submits Austria's application to join the EC.
	The Communist systems in Eastern Europe collapse. Fall of the Berlin wall.
1991	Armed conflict breaks out in Yugoslavia, Austria's neighbouring state starts to disintegrate.
1992	Dr. Thomas Klestil is elected Federal President.
1993	Dr. Heide Schmidt and four other deputies leave the FPÖ and found the Liberal Forum (LIF). Five parties are thus represented in the Austrian Parliament.
1993	International Human Rights Conference in Vienna.
1994	66.93 per cent of Austrians vote to join the EU.
1995	General election and federal election in Styria.
1996	Waltraud Klasnic (ÖVP) is the first woman to become Provincial Governor of a federal province (Styria).
1997	Dr. Franz Vranitzky resigns as Federal Chancellor and is succeeded by Mag. Viktor Klima.
1998	Austria is highly successful at the Winter Olympic Games in Japan in February.
	In March Austria is one of eleven countries to introduce the Euro in its starting phase.
1998	Participation in the Schengen Agreement means the end of frontier checks with Germany and Italy and tougher controls along the outside borders of the EU.
	Dr. Thomas Klestil is re-elected Federal President.

Vienna

Beneath the spire of St. Stephen's, in front of the Chapel of St. Catherine, a slab is set into the stone floor of the Cathedral. Unnoticed by many visitors, it denotes the site of "the coordinate source for the royal and imperial land register survey of 1817 — 1837". The precise survey point is indicated by an isosceles triangle with a point in the centre — it lies exactly in the extension of the rod on the spire, not as it stands today, but as it was calculated in 1817; since then subsidence has caused considerable displacement. This detracts nothing from the slab's symbolism nor from the events of 1817. St. Stephen's Cathedral, the starting-point for a survey of Austria (far beyond the borders of today's Republic), is the centre of the federal capital. Once an imperial capital and the residence of rulers, the city has remained an independent federal province since the fall of the Habsburg monarchy. St. Stephen's is "Austria's Cathedral": after the Second World War, when vast areas of Vienna lay in ruins and the Cathedral itself was devastated, the Austrian people's will to rebuild and their realistic optimism were best summed up by a popular and slightly sentimental song, its subject this very Cathedral, or "Steffl", as it is affectionately known.

Vienna is not Austria, however, no more than Paris is France nor Rome Italy. As far as early settlement is concerned — the earliest traces indicate a period some eight thousand years ago — the Danube metropolis is certainly a match for other parts of Austria. In Roman times, however, as from the early first century after the birth of Christ, Vindobona ranked well below Carnuntum further down the Danube. Even in the Middle Ages, Idrisi, an Arabian scholar and globe-trotter, found Krems more worthy of detailed description as a trading centre than the Vienna of those days. Austria's oldest extant church does not stand in the federal capital, but in Linz; experts are not agreed as to which was the oldest castle on Austrian soil, but it was not a Viennese building. Vienna even succeeded in disappearing from the pages of history for considerable periods of time: in 433 Rome ceded "Pannonia prima", of which Vienna was a part, to the Huns; a "Dark Age" followed until the Lombards took possession and the subsequent period until Charlemagne's wars with the Avars is again partially obscure. In around 550, Jordanes, the Ostrogoth, mentioned "Vindomina" as the remotest of the Pannonian towns — how did the change in name come about? Not until the Salzburg annals of 881 is there any further reference, mention being made in that year of a "bellum cum Ungaris ad Weniam", although it is not clear whether this refers to the town itself or to the river.

But what would a city like Vienna be without its conundrums, unusual as they always are. The origins of its name are still uncertain. According to current expert opinion, it most probably derives from the rivulet Vedunia, now known as the Wienfluss; it is more familiar to many Viennese as the river running alongside the western approach to the city than as an autonomous watercourse. Beside the "Theater an der Wien" the river is no longer visible, being arched in and covered by the Naschmarkt. Beethoven composed *Fidelio* for that theatre, but with true Viennese logic the best-known feature of the building is not, as one might expect, called the "Leonore portal", but the "Papageno gate" — not in homage to Mozart, but in memory of Emanuel Schikaneder, who wrote the libretto of *The Magic Flute* and who commissioned the building of the theatre, opened in 1801. It does contain a memorial plaque to Beethoven, not as a reminder of his opera, but of his violin concerto. "See what I mean?", as the real Viennese would say, if there is such a thing as a real Viennese and that, too, is uncertain.

What is certain is that historic Vienna is identical with the first district of today, that district called "Vienna — Inner City" and lately known as the "City". But any comparison with the business quarter of London is unconvincing: the Stock Exchange might be located within the Ringstrasse, but the Bank of Austria is situated in the ninth district.

Back to historic Vienna. It acquired its muni-

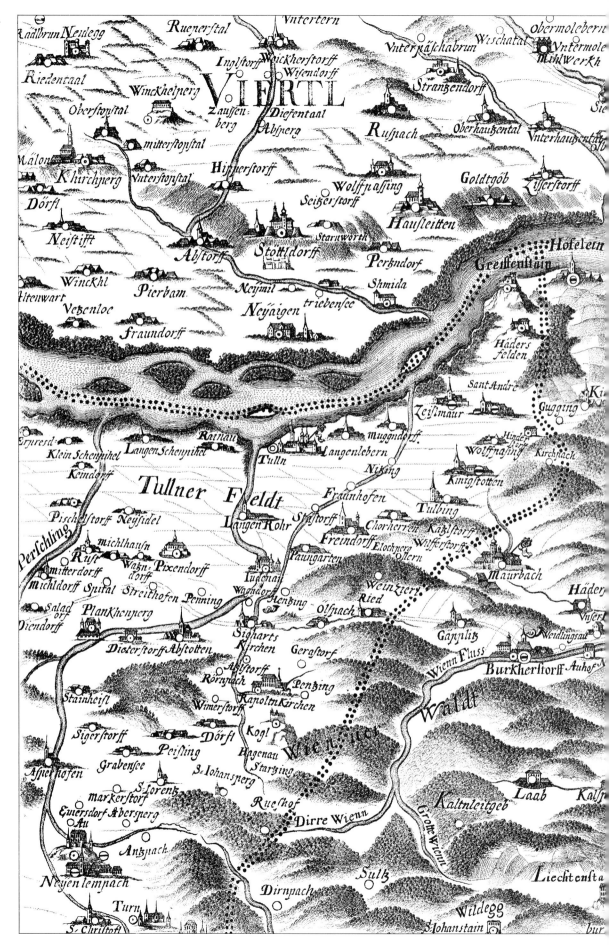

Vienna and surroundings,
G. M. Vischer, 1669.

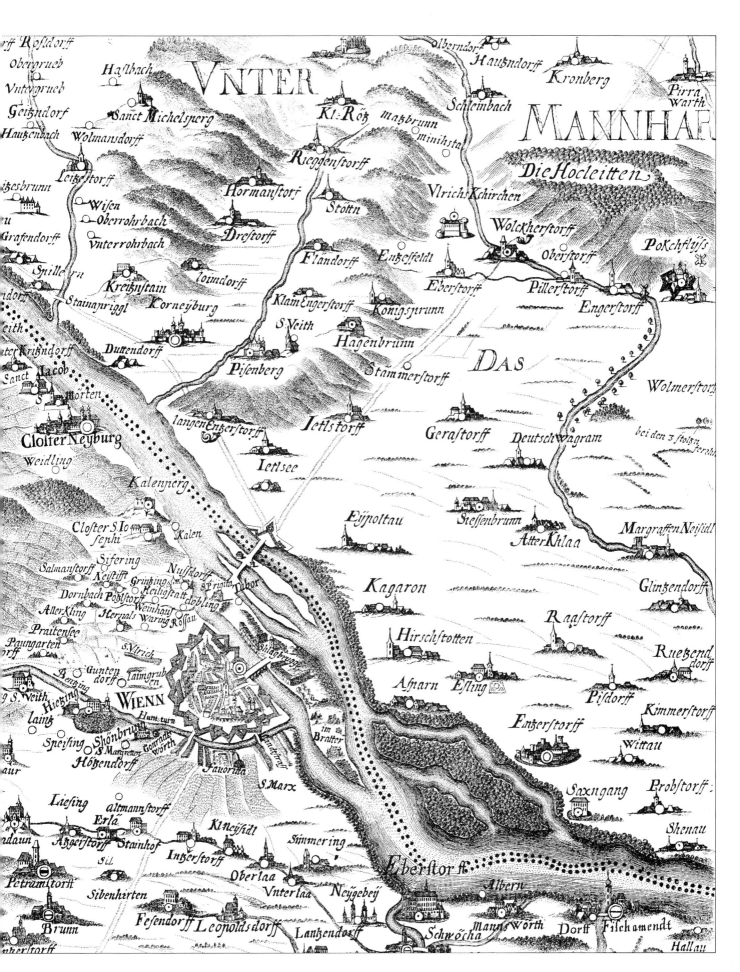

cipal charter in 1296, the first such document to be written in German and not in Latin. However, the very first civic rights were granted to the Danube metropolis in 1221 — it was already termed "civitas", or "town", in 1137 — and under Frederick the Quarrelsome, the Babenberg who ruled from 1230 until his death in 1246, Vienna was at times subject to the emperor alone, but it only enjoyed this privilege for a brief period.

Earlier still it had been the residence of princes: in around 1155 the Babenberg Henry II "Jasomirgott" transferred his seat from Klosterneuburg to Vienna, choosing today's Am Hof as the site of his palace. This must have been an important centre of politics and of music for it was at the Court of Vienna that Walther von der Vogelweide learnt "song and saga". The Hofburg of today was built later: historians attribute its foundations to Ottokar II of Bohemia, but there is a theory that the Babenbergs were, in fact, responsible. However that may be, whereas St. Stephen's is indisputably the spiritual centre of the city, the Hofburg and its surroundings remain the temporal focus. The Head of State has his official residence here and the Federal Chancellery is just opposite. Emperor Franz Joseph's monumental project was never carried out, of course, and the Neue Hofburg only forms one of the two semicircles originally planned; instead of the other half, the view in the direction of Parliament has the Rathaus and the Burgtheater as its focal point.

Perfectionism is not one of Vienna's traits. The paramount example of this is St. Stephen's itself: it only boasts one steeple, the "Steffl"; the second has remained a torso and that is what makes it so characteristic. Incidentally, major sections of the Cathedral were donated by Viennese citizens. When building work commenced in the twelfth century, the church was not even in the town, but outside its walls which ran along the boundary of the former Roman camp. The Romans can still be traced, of course, not, strictly speaking, in the town, but beneath it: objects found are presented in the form of a museum below ground level at the Platz am Hof and on the Hoher Markt.

The latter are among the most remarkable squares in Vienna, a delight to visitors in spite of the traffic chaos and the underground car park. Am Hof was where Pope Pius VI blessed the people in 1782 and where Francis II laid down the imperial crown of the Holy Roman Empire in 1806, the Austrian Empire having been proclaimed in 1804. A graceful column of the Virgin Mary provides a reminder of the Swedish menace, averted at the end of the Thirty Years War. In the Hoher Markt is the fountain of St. Joseph; the historic figures which parade at noon on the nearby Anker Clock range from Marcus Aurelius to Joseph Haydn. Both squares have witnessed lively market activity — the old "Christkindlmarkt" used to be held Am Hof — and a joyous hustle and bustle ever since the days of the minnesingers. But both — although this is a tale not so readily told to visitors — were also the scene of bloody assizes. Three mayors of Vienna were executed here for high treason, whatever that may have meant in the respective situation: Konrad Vorlauf on the 11th June, 1408 because he supported the wrong man at the wrong moment, the men in question being Ernst and Leopold, the feuding Habsburg brothers; Wolfgang Holzer on 14th April, 1463 for a similar reason and, on 11th August, 1522, Martin Siebenbürger who showed too much self-assurance when confronting the regime of Charles V and Ferdinand I. Other differences between the "imperial city" of Vienna and the wearers of the crown had a less tragic outcome, but they occurred again and again. Franz Joseph repeatedly refused to confirm Karl Lueger's election as Mayor of Vienna. In 1897, when Lueger's Christian Socialists had long held a two thirds majority in the town, the monarch was forced to give

Vienna, Schönbrunn, copper engraving by G. M. Vischer, Topographia Archiducatus Austriae Inf. 1672.

DER KHAISERLICHE LVST und THIERGARTEN SCHENBRVNN

VIENNA·PANNONIE

way. Today, two traffic areas in the first district bear the name of that popular politician: the section of the Ring at the University and the square at the end of the Wollzeile, containing Lueger's monument. Nicknamed "schöne Karl", or "handsome Charlie", Lueger made a metropolis of Vienna at the turn of the century. His memory is, however, clouded by his anti-Semitism, although it was socially motivated and had nothing in common with the bestiality of the Hitler era.

It was not, however, one of the city's mayors, but Emperor Franz Joseph who was responsible for what was perhaps the most decisive turning-point in Vienna's history. On 25th December, 1857 he ordered the "regulation and beautification of My city of residence and imperial capital". After the city walls had been demolished and the fortifications abandoned, as decreed in the Emperor's letter to Minister President Baron von Bach, this beautification culminated in the building of the Ringstrasse and the Franz-Josephs-Kai. It is useless to speculate what Vienna would look like, had there been a Board of Monuments at that time to protect the mediaeval ring walls, the projecting bastions and the predominantly Biedermeier — despite baroque buildings — character of the inner city. The city fathers were, in fact, of the opinion that the Emperor was not within his rights, the area in front of the fortifications not belonging to the State, but to the city; their objections were to no avail and, after all, the State financed the city extension fund.

The manifold styles of Historicism were chosen for the buildings, elements of the past being emulated and blended. Thus the only "authentic" building on the Ring is the Äussere Burgtor. Created in 1821—1824 to commemorate the Battle of Leipzig (1813), it could only be erected because Napoleon's troops had blown up the Burgbastei here in 1809, thus enabling the gardens of the Kaisergarten and Volksgarten to be laid out.

The oldest "Ringstrasse building" — in Vienna nothing is logical, not even chronology — was erected prior to the imperial decree, although not completed until 1879, and it is not actually situated on that magnificent road, even though visible from it: this is the Votivkirche with its filigree, neo-Gothic, twin-spired facade. Quite apart from being of architectural note, this building, like so many in the city, symbolizes events long past and personal tragedy: it was here that Niklas Count Salm, defender of Vienna in the face of the Turks in 1529, found his last resting place; the actual occasion for the building of the Votivkirche was Franz Joseph's life being spared in an attempted assassination in 1853, the initiator of the building project being the Emperor's younger brother, Maximilian of Mexico, who later met such an unhappy end. Salm's successor in the second Turkish siege of 1683, Rüdiger von Starhemberg, is buried inside the Schottenring, in the Benedictine monastery founded by Irish monks in 1155; an obelisk opposite the main University building, completed in 1884, commemorates Andreas

Northern view of the city of Vienna by Michel Wolgemut, pre-1493.

Liebenberg, Mayor of Vienna in 1683; with its magnificent baroque hall, the Old University on the Dr. Ignaz-Seipel-Platz harbours the Academy of Science. The original Alma Mater Rudolphina building (1365) no longer exists, but the old University quarter and the student dwellings in the area of the Jesuit Convent can still be clearly recognized. Originally (1554 to 1627) the Jesuits became established in the Kirche am Hof.

The image of Austria as a "monastery kingdom" is fully justified in Vienna, too, both in historic reminiscences and in the living present. Evidence is provided by the settlements of old monastic orders like the Dominicans (as from 1226) with their Church of "Maria Rotunda" and new sites like that of Mother Teresa of Calcutta's Missionaries of Charity. Seen in terms of the density of its churches, without exception the focal point of living communities, the city centre is equalled by few towns in the land.

Experts disagree as to which of the existing churches is the oldest in Vienna. According to current opinion, it is St. Peter's or, more precisely, a predecessor of that baroque edifice. A Roman hall church probably stood here originally. This would relegate the little Church of St. Rupert, an eleventh century building, to second place. Both have in common that their patron saints are linked with Salzburg, whereas St. Stephen's Cathedral is oriented to Passau, the mother diocese. Astonishingly, Vienna did not become a bishop's see until 1469 and an archdiocese until 1772. When it acquired its University in 1365, this did not originally have a Theological Faculty, a grave slight in comparison with other European universities.

When and where in the course of history Vienna and her citizens were slighted or, justifiably or not, felt themselves to be, could provide a subject for much philosophizing. But Viennese philosophizing has less to do with the great "love of wisdom" than with questions concerning the "last things", an interest in festive funerals and in the emotional proximity of death and gaiety, as besung in the wine taverns. Zurich, so goes the saying, is twice as big as the Central Cemetery of Vienna, but only half the fun. And few events can attract such a crowd to the Ringstrasse as a state funeral. Although at times it has been said ironically that the only sign of political

disturbance in Vienna is a diversion of traffic from the Ringstrasse to the "Zweierlinie" outer road.

So called after the "E2" and "H2" trams which once served the road running concentrically to the Ring, the "Zweierlinie" no longer exists. The road is now called the "Lastenstrasse", although a stranger looking this up in the list of streets will have no luck. Nor will he find anything under the collective term "Ring" — it is necessary to known the names of the various sections.

Nevertheless, the Ring remains one of the most representational and characteristic boulevards in the world or has again become so after the devastation of the Second World War. After all, this "nation of dancers and fiddlers", as Anton Wildgans, the poet, called them, started to rebuild the bombed out Burgtheater and the State Opera House at a time when misery and a shortage of housing were rife. In 1945 it was no longer remembered that the Opera House in particular had aroused such displeasure among the Viennese on its completion in 1869: August Siccard von Siccardsburg and Eduard van der Null, the architects, were regarded as lacking in style. The latter thereupon hanged himself and the former died shortly afterwards. Theophil von Hansen's Grecian inspired Parliament building, the Burgtheater by Gottfried Semper and Karl von Hasenauer, who also designed the Neue Hofburg and both large museums, Friedrich von Schmidt's neo-Gothic Town Hall, Heinrich Ferstel's University, emulating the Italian Renaissance, and the other eclectic buildings on the Ringstrasse only fared slightly better.

Outside, in the suburbs between the Ring and the Gürtel, the "Gründerzeit" buildings continued. And the suburbs long retained their village character, an intimation of which can still be sensed here and there on both sides of the Danube.

Not only is that river hardly ever blue, but until recently it was not even quite correct to place Vienna "on the Danube". It is only lately that the actual town has spread to the north bank, too; the Donauinsel has also played a part in bringing the Viennese and the great waterway together. The UN-City on the "other bank" still has something of an alien element, however, and Aspern and Essling, sites of Napoleonic battles in 1809 and now a part of

St. Stephen's is the focal point of Vienna and dates back to the 12th century. 137 m high, the south spire was completed in 1433 and is affectionately known as "Steffl". It has become the world famous symbol of the city.

Page 22/23:
a) View from St. Stephen's Cathedral across the rooftops of the inner city towards the Votivkirche and the new complex of the General Hospital.
b) Bowler-hatted coachmen with their fiacres await tourists at the Stephansplatz.
c) The Graben, an elegant shopping street and the centre of city life. Its name derives from Roman times when a moat (Graben) protected the Vindobona legionary camp here.
d) An unusual scene: a flurry of early-morning snow in the almost deserted Kohlmarkt.

22

c

d

a) Heldenplatz. Equestrian statues by Anton Fernkorn: Archduke Karl and Prince Eugene of Savoy; at the back, the Neue Burg; erected between 1881 and 1913 according to designs by Gottfried Semper and Carl von Hasenauer, this building was the final extension of the Hofburg complex.
b) Monument to Prince Eugene of Savoy; dome of the Kunsthistorisches Museum, also designed by Gottfried Semper and Carl von Hasenauer, 1872 to 1881.
c) The Spanish Riding School in the Hofburg and the white Lipizzaner stallions are world-famous symbols of Vienna.

Page 26/27:
a) The State Opera House, formerly the Court Opera House, was built in 1861 to 1869 according to plans by Eduard van der Nüll and August von Siccardsburg. After its destruction in the War it was rebuilt and the interior was redesigned.
b) The neo-Grecian Parliament, built by Theophil Hansen between 1873 and 1883. The Pallas Athene fountain in front of the main facade was designed by Karl Kundmann at the turn of the century; in the background, the Rathaus tower.
c) View of the Burgtheater from the terrace of Café Landtmann. Designed by Gottfried Semper and Carl von Hasenauer, the "Imperial Hofburg Theatre" opposite the Town Hall was opened in 1888.

b

c

a

b

The Lower Belvedere and the Upper Belvedere were erected in 1714 to 1716 and 1721 to 1723 respectively by Johann Lukas von Hildebrandt for Prince Eugene of Savoy. Hildebrandt's main work, this is regarded as one of the loveliest palaces in the world.
a) Sala terrena. b) View from the Upper to the Lower Belvedere and across the rooftops of Vienna with St. Stephen's Cathedral. c) South facade of the Upper Belvedere.

a) Summer morning in the Volksgarten.
b) Witnesses to Vienna's great artistic era: Karlsplatz station, built in 1898 by Otto Wagner; behind, the dome of the Karlskirche, the city's most notable baroque edifice (1716 to 1739) designed by Johann Bernhard Fischer von Erlach and his son, Joseph Emanuel.
c) House in the Linke Wienzeile, built in 1898 by Otto Wagner.

c

a) Palm-house dating to
Franz Joseph's day in the
palace grounds.
b) Carriage Museum,
imperial coach.
c) Schönbrunn Palace,
commenced in 1696
according to plans by
Johann Bernhard Fischer
von Erlach, remodelled
by Nikolaus Pacassi in
1744 to 1749 under
Empress Maria Theresa.
The gardens were laid
out by Jean Trehet.

a

b

c

d

a, b, c) The "Heurigen" wine gardens in the old wine growing village of Grinzing on the outskirts of the city are a favourite meeting place for the Viennese and an attraction for visitors.
d) Wine grower's cottage in Sievering.

View from the Reichs-
brücke to the UNO City,
a spacious conference
centre built in the Seven-
ties, the seat of various
international organiza-
tions.

the twenty second district, certainly do not derive their historic strength from being a part of the federal capital.

It is a little different in the case of the former suburbs in the south and west. They were incorporated in the precincts of Vienna after the second Turkish siege. On the suggestion of Prince Eugene, a rampart was erected, thirteen kilometres long, twelve feet high and wide, with a moat one and a half metres deep. It was demolished in 1894, most of the suburbs having been incorporated in the city in 1890. Some of the old "rampart office" buildings still stand, although the historic connection is no longer familiar to our contemporaries. Local traditions are, however, being revived again in the old hamlets; quite a few of these once independent manors go back to the tenth and early twelfth century.

One of these is Hietzing, the thirteenth district. Like Währing (Vienna XVIII) and Döbling (Vienna XIX), it includes large residential areas and is regarded as a "posh area", although this is mainly on account of Schönbrunn Palace being located there. Everyone associates Schönbrunn with Vienna as an imperial city. The annual admissions are registered in seven figures, not including visitors to the zoo or people walking in the park, but this influx is unfortunately not beneficial to the historic apartments.

That is why a project has been developed to put the management of the entire site — it has belonged to the Republic since the fall of the Monarchy — into private hands, giving it a more professional care than it received from the various ministries. The idea has also been aired of renovating the Neugebäude Renaissance palace in the east of the city and of making it attractive for foreign visitors to Vienna, thereby relieving Schönbrunn.

Hitherto Vienna has not really been associated

Vienna, overall view, copper engraving by Antoine Aneline, 1723.

VIENNE EN AUTRICHE

DANUBE FLEUVE

with the Renaissance. The Schweizertor of the Hofburg and the Stallburg with its arcaded courtyard are familiar, but primarily as the entrance to the Treasury and as the home of the Lipizzaners. The Gothic style is hardly thought of in connection with Vienna either, except in the case of St. Stephen's. In fact, many buildings of worth outside the former city walls were destroyed in the Turkish Wars of 1529 and 1683; others, particularly in the centre, were intrinsically altered by baroquification. Vienna would, however, be unthinkable without gems like Maria am Gestade, the Augustinian Church or the Minorite Church. But, all in all, Vienna is regarded as a city of baroque and Biedermeier. Baroque buildings dominate, if only on account of their monumentality, be they churches or palaces, and perhaps because they date back to the age of Austrian heroes. In general the Viennese are not characterized by their heroic qualities, but there is no denying their pluck or their staying-power. They demonstrated that after 1945 and it is perhaps no mere coincidence that Prince Eugene's Belvedere should have been chosen as the site of the most auspicious event in Austria's recent history, the ratification of the State Treaty on 15th May, 1955.

In very recent years *fin de siècle* Vienna has been rediscovered, particularly *art nouveau,* although at the time the Viennese did not know what to make of it. Again, the tendency towards morbidity and the attraction of death come to mind: among the most powerful sacred buildings of that epoch are the church at Steinhof Psychiatric Hospital — it was known bluntly as the madhouse when Otto Wagner built it between 1904 and 1907 — and the church in the Central Cemetery, erected soon afterwards. Even today there is little understanding for the fact that international groups of architects come to view the Werkbund estate in the Lainz cottage area and the Karl-Marx-Hof in Heiligenstadt, the architectonic epitome of Social Democratic ideology between the Wars, which has acquired the character of a monument.

Vienna has its problems with the present, too, of course — what city does not? Hollein's Haas House and the Hrdlicka monument are two striking examples, so is the Hundertwasser House. But it is no longer the case that those who cherish historic buildings are regarded as old-fashioned or those open-minded to modern architecture as totally mad. This does not only apply to architecture. After all, in the Musikverein — its Goldener Saal is regarded as the loveliest concert hall in the world, just as Fischer von Erlach's National Library is regarded as the loveliest room of its kind — twentieth century works no longer have to be embedded between Mozart and Beethoven to stop the audience running away. And, after all, modern art has its museums alongside the great traditional houses. Whether and when the new project for the "loveliest museum island in the world" will come about remains to be seen.

The prospect of Vienna one day becoming one huge museum is not to be feared — if only because one cannot visualize the city's population as custodians one and all. That much quoted phrase "Vienna remains Vienna" — some critics say this is an implicit threat — could prove true. At least, if the term "Vienna" includes Vindobona and Vidomina, Wenia and Wienne.

Pia Maria Plechl

Vienna comprises 415 km² of which 324 km² is a permanent settlement area with approximately 1,540,000 inhabitants.

DISTRICTS

  I. Innere Stadt
 II. Leopoldstadt
III. Landstraße
 IV. Wieden
  V. Margareten
 VI. Mariahilf
VII. Neubau
VIII. Josefstadt
 IX. Alsergrund
  X. Favoriten
 XI. Simmering
XII. Meidling
XIII. Hietzing
XIV. Penzing
 XV. Rudolfsheim-
     Fünfhaus
XVI. Ottakring
XVII. Hernals
XVIII. Währing
XIX. Döbling
 XX. Brigittenau
XXI. Floridsdorf
XXII. Donaustadt
XXIII. Liesing

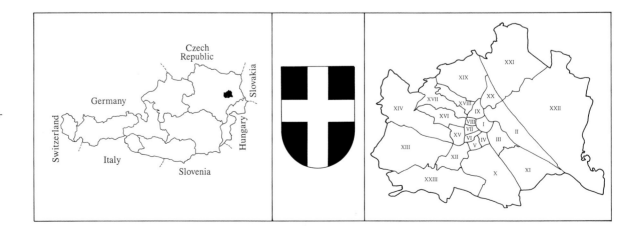

Lower Austria

"In the name of the holy and undivided Trinity. Otto, by divine predestined indulgence Emperor and Ruler of the Kingdom. May the zeal of all our loyal followers . . . know that we . . . have conferred certain properties to which we have title in the tract of land commonly know as OSTAR-RICHI, in the Mark and County of Count Heinrich, the son of Margrave Luitpald, in the place called Neuhofen, to the bosom of Freising Church . . .".

Thus runs that document of 1st November, 996 in which the name "Österreich" was first mentioned. This "Ostarrichi" is Lower Austrian land and Neuhofen an der Ybbs regards itself as the cradle of Austria, having its commemorative site and celebrating its anniversaries. Are the Lower Austrians, therefore, the original Austrians? Yes and no. They are in name, they are as inhabitants of that land which became the heart of the Habsburg monarchy by way of unification with Styria (1192) and more than ever after Rudolf of Habsburg's victory over Ottokar of Bohemia (1278). But Austrian history is also what happened in the other federal provinces of today and historians from the southern and western areas of the country rightly object to Lower Austria's monopolization.

Be that as it may, the red, white and red Austrian shield comes from the land below the Enns. It is highly probable that this shield was borne by the Counts of Poigen; Wildberg Castle to the north-west of Horn nurtures this tradition. Documentary evidence shows that the shield was the Babenberg coat of arms in 1230, but it was actually in use much earlier, the oldest state symbol of its kind in Europe.

A province today and a duchy and county for centuries prior to that, Lower Austria bears the blue and gold "lark" emblem. The larks are, in fact, eagles, but what does it matter? It is perhaps characteristic of that race of people along the Danube, in the forests of the north and in the mountains of the south, that they reduce lofty claims to power to the familiar, at the same time heroizing that which is simple. Initially the Babenberg eagle was the imperial eagle, borne from 1156 on, whereas the red, white and red shield originally only possessed local significance, becoming a symbol of bravery due to a legend. Leopold V, so it is told, fought so bravely during the Crusade at Acre that his tunic became soaked in blood, only remaining white in the area covered by his belt. The legend does not stand up to historical scrutiny, but it lives on. After all, as well as being good sovereigns, most of the Babenbergs were valiant, not just their most famous son, Margrave Leopold the Holy (1095 to 1136). It was his outstanding political feat to have prevented a battle between Henry IV, the Holy Roman Emperor, and the Emperor's son, an admirable achievement for which Leopold was rewarded with the hand of Agnes, the daughter and sister of an emperor.

Important as the Babenbergs might have been in the making of Lower Austria, the name of a second dynasty, the mightiest after the rulers, is mentioned more frequently today — the Kuenringers. In recent years a notable campaign has been waged to defend their honour. The reasons for this are highly realistic, for these Kuenringers — who today associates them with the tiny Waldviertel hamlet of Kühnring? — were not merely, not even mainly, unruly robber barons. Their share in building castles and monasteries of renown was great — Aggstein and Zwettl are the most outstanding examples.

Zwettl is one of those ecclesiastical institutions that have helped to give Austria, and, in particular, Lower Austria, the name of a "monastery kingdom". Nearly all these strongholds of God go back to the Babenberg era, the Cistercian houses being situated in the plains, by rivers and streams, the Benedictine abbeys proudly commanding the heights. In their baroque splendour with Gothic elements and Romanesque vestiges, they still determine the character of the province and they are outstanding works of art. Greatest among them is Melk where canons already resided in the castle built after 976. They were followed by Benedictines in 1089. Between 1702 and 1726 Jakob Prandtauer, in consummate accord with

Abbot Berthold Dietmayr, created the monastery of today. One of the most notable sacred buildings in Europe, it is a masterpiece which employed practically every notable artist of the age.

Had Johann Lukas von Hildebrandt, the architect, had his way, Göttweig — founded as an abbey of Augustinian canons in 1074 by Bishop Altmann of Passau, it passed to the Benedictines in 1094 — would have surpassed even Melk Abbey. The plan was triumphal, but was only realized in part. Nevertheless Göttweig is an overall work of art, rich in art treasures and in living spiritual tradition.

Unfinished — is that a Lower Austrian fate? And yet, Klosterneuburg is splendid, too. Founded before 1108 on the site of the Roman settlement of Asturis, it was transformed into a Babenberg residence by Leopold III and consigned to the Augustinian canons. Emperor Charles VI wished to create an Austrian Escorial here. Jakob Prandtauer submitted a design, the construction was the work of Donato Felice d'Allio, much influenced by Fischer von Erlach the younger, and was completed by Josef Kornhäusel. Nothing could express the claim more eloquently than the Holy Roman Emperor's crown and the Austrian Archducal cap on the domes of the abbey. The church is not only the final resting place of Leopold the Holy, it also harbours one of the province's most outstanding works of art, the altar created by Nikolaus of Verdun in 1181. Its enamel panels depict the relationship between pre-Mosaic and post-Mosaic history and the life of Christ.

As in Klosterneuburg, the cloisters and the fountain constitute a major element in the Cistercian Abbey of Heiligenkreuz, founded by Leopold III in 1135/36. Baroque additions were made, but the imposing church has retained its Romanesque-Gothic character. The burial site of Friedrich II, the last Babenberg, Heiligenkreuz was where Raphael Donner, the sculptor, created his earliest works. It is the mother abbey of Zwettl and Lilienfeld; the former was a Kuenringer foundation (1137), renewed in baroque style after 1722 by Matthias Steinl and Josef Munggenast, the latter (founded 1219) includes the first hall church in Austria. Since the baroque renovation it has also been famous as the site of Daniel Gran's altar showing the Assumption.

Herzogenburg (founded in 1112 and transferred to its present site in 1244), Geras (1150), Altenburg (1144) and Kleinmariazell (1136) must be mentioned in connection with the "monastery kingdom", so must Dürnstein or the Benedictine monastery of St. Pölten founded in 760, its name a local abbreviation of St. Hippolytus.

Today, Lower Austria numbers some thirty monasteries. Among the younger establishments is St. Gabriel in Maria Enzersdorf, the seat of the Steyl Missionaries since 1889. In the course of his reforms Joseph II dissolved about fifty conventual houses, one of them being the collegiate foundation of Ardagger (1049) with the oldest stained glass windows in Austria. Mariabrunn, which now belongs to Vienna, did not, however, fall victim to that Emperor of the Enlightenment, but existed until 1829. The Charterhouses of Mauerbach and Gaming were, on the other hand, affected; both had links with the Habsburg, Frederick the Handsome.

Lower Austria was not shaped solely by the houses of God-fearing men and women, however. Of all the provinces it has the greatest number of towns and market communes of which there were thirty seven and two hundred and twenty respectively as long ago as the late Middle Ages. Five hundred castles, strongholds and similar buildings have been preserved; add to this some one hundred and fifty ruins and the last traces of nearly five hundred fortresses, and these figures can hardly be equalled.

Not a few of these castles once stood sentinel along the great routes, two of which date back to the earliest history of the area. The Danube and the road that soon followed its banks, the *limes* of the Roman period, predominate, together with the prehistoric amber road and the north-south routes from the Waldviertel via Krems to the Traisental, and from Brno via Laa and Baden to Steinamanger. Only the Semmering remained unused as a pass road by the Romans: until the eleventh and twelfth century the "Cerwald" was regarded as impassable, not until the thirteenth century did it become known as the route taken by Ulrich von Liechtenstein, the minnesinger (1227).

The province's links with art, music and literature are older. Sculpture goes back to the period around 40,000 BC, the earliest known item being the famous "Venus of Willendorf".

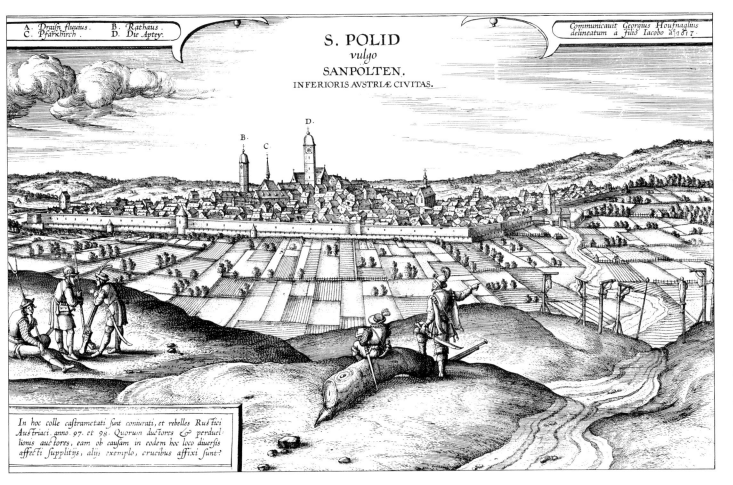

St. Pölten, copper engraving by Jacob Hufnagel, from Braun and Hogenberg's "Städtebuch", 1617.

The oldest cult sculpture in local primeval history, its form indicates a fertility symbol. On the other hand, the "dancing Venus" found fairly recently (1988) and created in c. 30,000 BC is characterized by an elegance of line. And in the last ten thousand years of pre-Christian prehistory and protohistory the people who settled here fashioned a wealth of ceramic designs. Numerous excavated items bear witness to this.

With the Romans came a new culture which left an impressive amount of evidence along the Danube and elsewhere, too. For a long time the capital of Pannonia, frequently the destination of emperors, Carnuntum is the outstanding example. It was here that Marcus Aurelius, philosopher enthroned, wrote his "Meditations". Some of the most beautiful parts can be read on the commemorative stone in Deutsch-Altenburg park:

"Men who do not heed the motions of their own soul must of necessity be unhappy",

"From eternity all things come to pass in the same way"

and, finally, "The duration of human life is a moment, the essence is a steady current".

From here the Romans again and again moved north across their bridges with varying success. For the *limes* frontier marked the confines of the Roman Empire, but not of Roman influence. And the battle immortalized on the Marcus Aurelius Column in Rome took place north of the Danube — evidence of the Christians' loyalty to the Empire, however persecuted they were. In the closing days of the Roman Empire their faith was challenged by the cult of emperors and the worship of Mithras.

Two ancient saints with Lower Austrian links were also Romans, even though they did not come from the eternal city itself — Florian, a high official in what later became St. Pölten, and who was drowned in the Enns in the rule of Diocletian, and Severin whose path along the Danube was marked by the aid he gave to the local people, threatened by the Germans from the north. He settled in Mautern (Favianis) in 453, dying there in 482. Written by Eugippius, his pupil, his biography recounts a part of Lower Austria's history. Many of his Romanized contemporaries left the area as the Roman Empire began to crumble, taking his body with them on their way south.

Culture was not just a Roman prerogative. One of the most notable finds, now housed in the Kunsthistorisches Museum in Vienna, is Germanic: the "treasure of the lame princess of Untersiebenbrunn", a German who died with her child in the Marchfeld. Her jewellery is among the loveliest to have been preserved from that era.

The princess came to the Lower Austria of today during the period of the *Völkerwanderung,* but the landscape between the lower Alps and the Thaya, between the Enns and the March was always territory that invited people to traverse it and to settle there. It has remained so. It witnessed Illyrians and Celts, Romans and Germans, Huns and Avars, those mounted warriors from the east, Slavs from the king-dom of Great Moravia and those who came later, Bavarians and Germanic tribes, the Bohemians of Ottokar (who cannot, of course, be considered in nationalistic terms), down to the Croats at the time of the Turkish peril or the refugees of our century who have made their homes here. All those who remained were assimilated fairly quickly: Lower Austria is not a province of minorities and, even if there are a wide variety of dialects, the language remains uniform. After all, the first poetess of German tongue was a Lower Austrian or lived here as a recluse at the foot of Melk — Frau Ava, who died in 1127. And it is asserted that Walther von der Vogelweide, the most famous of all minnesingers, came from the Waldviertel, even though he is generally said to have been of South Tyrolean extraction. He certainly learnt "song and saga" in Vienna

Klosterneuburg, copper engraving by H. G. Bodenehr, c. 1690.

Newstatt.

which for most of its history was indeed the capital of the country, the centre for all four districts above and below the Vienna Woods and above and below the Manhartsberg. The land below the Enns has recently acquired a provincial capital again, the only such capital in Austria to have been chosen democratically. As yet it is not fully functioning; it will take a while for the Lower Austrians to become fully accustomed to St. Pölten as a seat of government. Lower Austria's historic *Landhaus* remains in the Herrengasse in Vienna, of course. Ecclesiastically, the division into the archdiocese of Vienna and the diocese of St. Pölten remains. The people of Wiener Neustadt have not forgotten the era (1469 to 1784) during which a bishop resided within their walls. This became obvious after 1969, when the South Viennese vicariate acquired its first see there, an auxiliary bishop moving to the former see of a diocese. His successor as vicar is the parish priest of Baden and the Church of St. Stephen in the old spa town has thus been upgraded — and not merely by chance.

Baden and Wiener Neustadt: their similarities and their differences characterize much that determines Lower Austria and, *mutatis mutandis,* that is repeated in other parts of the province. Baden is an ancient settlement area: it gave its name to a neolithic culture. The Romans appreciated its hot springs, calling it "Aquae"; in 869 King Karlmann held court "ad Padun". Wiener Neustadt was founded at a strategically vital point in 1194 and was financed from part of the ransom paid for Richard the Lionheart. It acquired its

municipal charter in 1277, Baden having to wait for its charter until 1480 during the rule of Emperor Frederick III. He resided for a time in the castle at Wiener Neustadt, a place that remained "ever true" to him even in those difficult years of confrontation with Matthias Corvinus. Wine and spa activities have remained Baden's main points of emphasis down through the centuries, whereas Wiener Neustadt has developed into an industrial town. In 1848, the year of revolutions, Baden was one of the few towns to remain loyal both to the Emperor and to Metternich, who owned a house there, and it has retained its middle class loyalties. Wiener Neustadt soon became a bulwark of Social Democracy and that has not changed either. During the Second World War it was almost totally destroyed by more than fifty thousand bombs in twenty nine air raids and it held the sorry record of being Austria's most damaged town. Baden acquired sad renown after the War as the headquarters of the Soviet force of occupation.

The War and its aftermath took a greater toll in Lower Austria than in any other Austrian province. As so often in the course of history, it was a scene of warfare in 1945, and the damage suffered during the occupation can hardly be measured: the keeps and castles fell victim to senseless devastation and wild plundering, local people taking a greater part in this than many would care to believe.

The most distinguished example of destruction and revival stands for many others — the Schallaburg, Lower Austria's exhibition site *par excellence.* It became internationally

Wiener Neustadt, copper engraving by Matthäus Merian, Topographia Austriae 1649.

renowned thanks to its terracotta courtyard commissioned by Hans Wilhelm von Losenstein (1546 to 1601), the epitome of a Lower Austrian gentleman of rank during the Renaissance. Classically educated, culturally influenced by a tour of Italy, he was of Protestant faith, like most of his compeers in the area before the House of Habsburg initiated the recatholicization. The adaptation of the building from a late eleventh century castle to an elegant residence — still ready to defend itself — was characteristic of the era. In the second half of the nineteenth century the Schallaburg belonged to Karl Wilhelm, Baron Tinti. He was a philanthropist and the first president of the Austrian Red Cross Society, a circumstance paralleled in the humanitarian work of many a Lower Austrian castle owner.

During the Second World War the Schallaburg was sold — independently of any political considerations — to a German aristocrat, a relative of the later Cardinal Count Galen who spoke out against the murder of the sick and the handicapped. As "German property" it became caught up in a legalistic labyrinth in 1945; held by the Soviet force of occupation, it was devastated beyond belief by soldiers and their local friends. Ten years after the ratification of the State Treaty it was still an object of negotiation. The fact that the owner had meanwhile become an Austrian did not simplify matters, but paradoxically complicated them. The first restoration work was undertaken during the period when the legal situation was still uncertain. Finally the Province of Lower Austria was able to acquire the site for a token sum from the Austrian Republic which meanwhile owned it. In 1974 restoration work was completed; many an architectural gem had been discovered. The Losensteiner tomb returned home and the Provincial Exhibition on the Renaissance became the first of a long series of cultural presentations to be held at the Schallaburg.

Later, equally auspiciously, restoration work on the two loveliest Marchfeld castles, Schlosshof and Niederweiden, entered its decisive phase. Since the days of Prince Eugene they have been linked with one another. Made famous by Canaletto's painting and surrounded by vast grounds, Schlosshof was built for that Prince of Savoy between 1725 and 1729 by Lukas von Hildebrandt who incorporated the old fortified castle. Maria Theresa had it enlarged; since the era of Joseph II it has served manifold purposes, recently having been a military institution for the training of riders and drivers. Memories had already long faded of those baroque festivities at which gilded leaves and marzipan fruit hung from the trees and the play of fountains alternated with theatrical performances. Its beauty could still be imagined, however, despite indescribable devastation. The partial restoration was not completed until the Prince Eugene Exhibition in 1986. There is still much to be done, but year for year the energetic Society for the Preservation of the Marchfeld Castles prevents its relapsing into a Sleeping Beauty slumber.

The same applies to Niederweiden, the most charming of Fischer von Erlach's palaces, built for Starhemberg, Vienna's defender against the Turks in 1683, and then acquired by Prince Eugene. Restoration work commenced earlier here, but no sooner had it begun than the little castle fell victim to a fire in 1956. Even after restoration, the enchanting building with its illusionist paintings (Jean Pillement) in the oval banqueting hall still lacked a purpose. Now annual exhibitions are held there, preventing the hunting lodge of Niederweiden from going to waste as its predecessor, Grafenweide Castle, did after the fifteenth century when its unlawful owners were executed as robber knights. Both the elegant main building and the game kitchen of yore are becoming an object of increasing interest. The kitchen, or rather the cuisine, provides one of the attractions in the Riegersburg, that magnificent baroque edifice in the Waldviertel, hard by the border with the Czech Republic which cuts it off from its historic hinterland. That an "aristocratic nineteenth century country house" has been furnished here is to the credit of the Khevenhüller heirs and of Franz Windisch-Graetz, the Viennese art historian. Here and in Petronell on the Danube, seat of the Counts of Abensberg and Traun since 1656, he realized his idea of a castle museum jointly run by private ownership and public collections.

While we are on the subject of castle museums in Lower Austria, Austria's greatest and most outstanding art collection at once comes to mind — the "Count Harrach Family Collection" at Rohrau Castle in the place of the same name. It is the birthplace of Haydn, his home has been furnished as a memorial site and is

Girls in Wachau costume
at harvest thanksgiving in
Spitz an der Donau.

a

b

The Wachau, where the
Danube Valley is at its
loveliest:
a) Dürnstein and the
former Augustinian
priory.
b) View over the peach
trees on the right bank of
the Danube across to
Schwallenbach.
c) The Benedictine
Abbey of Melk, built in
1702 to 1726 by Jakob
Prandtauer.

47

St. Pölten, the capital of Lower Austria: a) right, the tower of the Town Hall (1571 to 1591), left, the spire of the Prandtauer Church (formerly the Church of Carmelite Nuns, 1712).
b) Herrenplatz and column of the Virgin Mary.
c) Rathausgasse and Town Hall (far right).

b

c

49

A variety of superb period pieces:
a) Apostle group from the late Gothic altar-piece in Mauer Parish Church near Melk.
b) Terracotta courtyard, 1573, by Jakob Bernecker in the Schallaburg near Melk.
c) Cloisters (mid-13th cent.) in Lilienfeld Collegiate Church.
d) Ceiling fresco (1748/1749 acc. to design by Daniel Gran) in the chancel of Herzogenburg Collegiate Church.
e) The cloisters (1220 to 1250) at Heiligenkreuz Abbey; this is the earliest Cistercian foundation in the Babenberg era.

Page 52/53: The atmosphere that marked the spa of Baden's heyday as an imperial summer residence can still be sensed today: a) autumn in the Vienna Woods, b) trotting racecourse, c) promenade concert, d) morning mood in the Doblhoffpark.

e

c

d

Weinviertel scenes:
a) Harvesting marrows near Zellerndorf.
b, c) Fertile land as far as the eye can see: at Großnondorf (b) and Zistersdorf (c).

Page 56/57:
a, c) Vineyard and "Heurigen" garden in Sooß at the foot of the Vienna Woods.
b) Field of poppies at Zwettl in the Waldviertel.
d) The old house fronts at Drosendorf in the uppermost Waldviertel are lovingly cared for.

c

d

57

The apse of Schön-
grabern Parish Church
(13th cent.). Dedicated to
the Virgin Mary, the
church is an extraordi-
nary monument to the
Romanesque on account
of its sculptural deco-
ration.

Page 59:
a, b) The ruins of the
Roman town of Carnun-
tum in Petronell; right,
the early 4th cent.
"Heathens' Arch".
c) A gathering storm near
Gänserndorf.

A detail from the "Verdun Altar" in the Leopold chapel at Klosterneuburg Abbey. The enamel work was created in 1181 by Nicolas of Verdun.

an attraction in itself. Haydn's links with the Harrach family serve as an example of intelligent patronage in the province. Another reminder is the bust of Haydn in the castle, since 1970 the home of the gallery previously housed in the Harrach palace on the Freyung in Vienna. The beauty of this collection — mainly composed of Spanish and Italian masterpieces, it also includes the famous "Three ladies at their music", c. 1530, and the "Rohrauer Altar" from Antwerp — comes fully into its own in the ancient moated fortress which was later baroquified. In quality and abundance Rohrau is unrivalled in Lower Austria and indeed throughout Europe. The works of art in other keeps and castles — most of the buildings themselves masterpieces — are also deservedly extolled, however. The span is wide, wherever it starts or finishes. At Laxenburg, perhaps, that imperial palace whose heyday began after its devastation by the Turks in 1683. Franz I extended it, creating the Romantic, neo-Classical, neo-Gothic Franzensburg in which he installed the Capella speciosa from Klosterneuburg and the Renaissance wooden ceiling from Greillenstein. This latter is another of the great sights — on account of the actual building and the court museum. Via the "Ritterschaft auf blauer Erde" the link extends from Laxenburg to Seebenstein, a harbour of Gothic art. The love of Historicism was expressed in Grafenegg, the only example of an imitation of Tudor-Gothic in the English style, and it finds analogies in Kreuzenstein and in the Rosenburg which is "authentic" as only a building can be. Set high above the Kamp, with its tournament ground of yore and its thirteen towers, the Rosenburg was one of the "most distinguished castles in the entire land" and not just in the seventeenth century. At that time it was doubly famous due to its mention in a much-sung ballad on the subject of an innocent boy's death and owing to the bloody reality of the onslaught by Protestant estates in 1620. This cost three hundred men, women and children their lives.

Blood flowed again and again in the history of the castles and of the whole land, whether they were captured by foes or merely besieged, whether they fell prey to destruction or to cruel masters. Their numbers are legion, ranging — purely alphabetically — from Aggstein to Zelking, or from Raabs and Hardegg in the north to Kranichberg and Steyersberg in the

south, from the fortresses of the Waldviertel, like Rapottenstein or Ottenstein, to the castles along the Danube, from "Bechelarn" (Pöchlarn) of the *Nibelungenlied* to the ruin of Hainburg, already termed "ancient" in that thirteenth century work, from the fortifications south of the river — Gresten-Stiebar or Pottenbrunn, for instance — to the Museum of the Knights of Malta at Mailberg in the Weinviertel or to the castle of Asparn an der Zaya with its prehistoric museum, from fortresses perched on rocky crags, Starhemberg or the Araburg, to mighty citadels like Heidenreichstein. One and all they serve merely as examples.

They guarded routes and they commanded the land, they provided refuge for the oppressed in times of need and sometimes they were the strongholds of tyrants. Some of them were imbued with a whiff of European, even of world, history — Dürnstein, where Richard the Lionheart languished in 1193, a prisoner of Hadmar II of Kuenring; Orth, the property of Caroline, sister to Napoleon, widow of Murat; Eckartsau, a keep long since become a palace, where Charles, Emperor and King, renounced all share in the government of Hungary and from which he went into exile in 1919; Raabs, the lords of which were burgraves of Nuremberg, one of their daughters becoming the progenitrix of the House of Hohenzollern in the late twelfth century; Mayerling, scene of Crown Prince Rudolph's tragedy; and Artstetten with its tomb of Archduke Francis Ferdinand, the heir to the throne, and his wife.

It is perhaps only a legend that Napoleon, glimpsing the ruins of Rauheneck and Rauhenstein in the Helenental near Baden, remarked how pleasant it would be to grow old and to die in this "St. Helena". It is historical reality that the daughter of Louis XVI and Marie Antoinette, and after her Count Chambord, not only dreamed of restoring the old monarchy in France, but actually took steps to do so while living in Eichbüchl and Frohsdorf castle.

Fact or legend, these links with the "big wide world" are not restricted to castles and palaces alone. Is not Maria Lanzendorf said to have been the place where in 508 Prince Arthur of Britain found a mosaic stone indicating the presence of Luke the evangelist in AD 70? The story of the connection between the parish church and pilgrimage church of Deutsch-

Altenburg and King Stephen, the patron saint of Hungary (969 to 1038), seems more probable, the parish actually having been established prior to 1020.

Pilgrimage churches are of great importance for Lower Austria: from the sad ruin of Maria Raffingsberg, said to be the oldest pilgrimage site in the province, to the splendour of sacred places like Maria Taferl, the Mariahilf-Berg at Gutenstein, Maria Dreieichen, Unserfrau, Maria Schutz or Maria Laach; from the pilgrimage churches along the Via sacra connecting Vienna and Mariazell to relatively new examples like Dross or Stickelberg. For different reasons two must be emphasized: the Sonntagberg at Waidhofen an der Ybbs, where not the Virgin Mary, but the Holy Trinity is the object of veneration, and Maria Roggendorf near Hollabrunn. The renewal of its pilgrimage — the ancient pilgrimage was suspended by Joseph II — by Hans Hermann Groër, now Cardinal Archbishop of Vienna, made church history. Cardinal Karol Wojtyla, the Archbishop of Cracow, had agreed to lead a pilgrimage hither, but his election to the Papacy made it impossible for him to carry out his intention.

The number of pilgrimage places and religious monuments makes Lower Austria seem to be one of the most Roman Catholic of the Austrian provinces. And there is something in this despite the increasing secularization here, too. Where else can a huge, modern Barbara Cross be found in the middle of an oil drilling site? Where else is a church service for miners and metal workers celebrated underground, in the "grotto" at Hinterbrühl, site of Europe's largest subterranean lake?

Customs, both Christian and pagan, are alive in this land below the Enns. Annually at the summer solstice lights float down the March and the Danube, annually from church spires trumpeters proclaim the Lord's birth and the start of the New Year announcing, too, that the darkest season has passed its zenith. Popular Lower Austrian traditions are not as spectacular — nor such tourist attractions — as those in the Tyrol or the Salzkammergut, of course. But floral festivals by the Erlauf and Lunz lakes are impressive and harvest thanksgiving in a winegrowing area is certainly worth seeing.

Wine is a part of Lower Austria and it is no mere chance that it has its rightful place in Grillparzer's famous eulogy on the "good land". It is only in part correct that the Romans under Emperor Probus introduced the noble vine to the area: the Celts already practised viticulture along the Danube and though the Emperor merely permitted his veterans to attend to it, this was the deciding factor. Other details can be examined in the Wine Museum at Krems and in the new Wine College at the former monastery of Und.

Commended by the Council of Europe for the preservation of its old town, Krems has retained its significance of yore. In the twelfth century Idrisi, the Arabian scholar, marked this Krems on a map of the world, placing it before Vienna in order of importance. Here in very early days Gozzo, the town recorder who died in 1291, had a citadel built; here the "urbs chremisa" was mentioned in documents of 995; here Duke Albrecht II did honour to his house in 1349 when he ordered that the instigators of a Jewish persecution be severely punished; an indication of the town's affluence came in 1627 when Emperor Ferdinand II rebuked the people for "all manner of luxury and excess being pursued in apparel and in wassailing".

Neither Krems nor the Wachau area as a whole were spared the province's toils and tribulations; these included the Turkish peril in 1529, when Vienna was besieged for the first time, and the Thirty Years War, when the Swedes also pillaged Spitz, still one of the main Wachau centres today. After that prolonged struggle, after the Turkish threat had been banished in 1683, after the victory of Prince Eugene and after the plague died out at the beginning of the eighteenth century it was small wonder that the entire land rejoiced and that this *joie de vivre* found its triumphant expression in the baroque.

Was this why Lower Austria — still including Vienna — became, even remained, baroque? The new age — whether it commenced in the late eighteenth century under Maria Theresa with the foundation of the first industrial workers' estate, now a protected site, or decades later — encountered a receptive land. Sometimes too much so, as the demolition of Gothic doorways and old buildings shows — stones from the castle keep at Weitenegg were used for the construction of an ultramarine factory in 1870. However, the installation of the first Austrian railway line from Vienna to Deutsch-

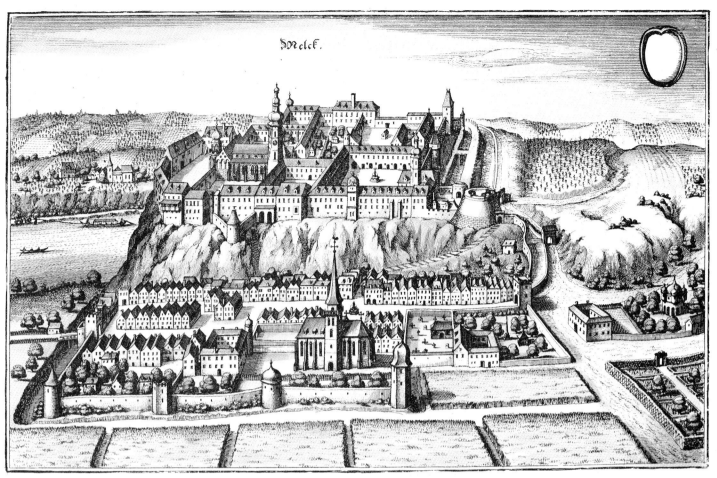

Wagram (1839), the second from Vienna to Mödling (1840) and, finally, the Semmering line (opened in 1854) — a European pioneering feat — signified milestones in European technology. The railway bridge opened at Marchegg in 1847 was still the one in greatest use throughout Europe in 1914. By 1829 the "K.k. privilegirte Erste Donaudampfschifffahrtsgesellschaft", the Danube Steamer Company, had been founded; one hundred years later the first successful petroleum drilling took place. Amazingly, this occurred in that north-eastern district in which, so the legend goes, there dwelt a rich, but hard-hearted race of dwarfs who sinned against a beggar, exclaiming, "Our gold shall turn to a black, foul-smelling pulp before we give you one single gram". Could that have been a presentiment of the "liquid gold" to come?

Parts of the scenery in the east are certainly characterized by the oil derricks and the people call them "locusts" without, however, meaning them to be a plague. South of the oilfields extends the Marchfeld, that ancient granary of the land of which Grillparzer said, "'tis a battlefield, yet a harvest field". It gave

its name to the great parade ground at the French officers' academy of St. Cyr — more a reminder of the battle of Wagram than of Essling where Napoleon was first defeated in 1809. Grillparzer was, of course, thinking of the confrontation between Ottokar and Rudolf von Habsburg. In the same drama Horneck declaims that eulogy on Austria which is a hymn of praise extolling Lower Austria, the silver ribbon of the Danube and the hills heavy with vines, the dark forest full of hunting pleasures and the blue-yellow of flax and saffron. Today, the great stretches of luminous yellow fields bear rape and are interspersed with acres of sugar-beet. The vineyards have changed their appearance since Grillparzer's day, but in the Wachau they do still rise in terraces. The Nordwald is no longer impassable as it was in the early nineteenth century. It has been opened up and the farmers, for many of whom agriculture is now merely an additional source of income, have been joined by more than a few townspeople. They have found a second home here in mills and farmsteads or in the towns, their squares and alleyways retaining many a mediaeval or baroque fea-

Melk, copper engraving by Matthäus Merian, Topographia Austriae 1649.

ture. The clear, cool Kamp has been dammed up into lakes which attract holidaymakers; the Danube, too, has been widened in parts in the interests of power generation — for a time this was the very symbol of economic prosperity and technological advance. The change in thought has been revealed most plainly in Lower Austria, in the "no" to the Zwentendorf atomic power plant in the Tullnerfeld and in the events surrounding the planned hydroelectric plant at Hainburg. This has brought fame to the Danube-March wetlands which hitherto were more or less unknown. In the foothills of the Alps and in the Alpine areas of the south rare or threatened animal and plant species are protected: the golden eagle and the marmots have their own habitat; high up on the Rax and Schneeberg edelweiss can be admired, but picking great numbers of them is no longer permitted.

The original home of Alpine skiing was in the Lower Austrian mountains, first the Lilienfeld area and then the Semmering. A fashionable ski resort in the period before and after the First World War, it has not quite overcome the consequences of the Second. At the turn of the century courageous local politicians saved the Vienna Woods from the encroaching city; today, mindful of pollution, their successors fear for the forest. The water, too, is threatened, the Mitterndorfer Senke only being one of many examples. Ecology and the environment were the greatest concern of one of Lower Austria's most famous men in our time — Konrad Lorenz, the Nobel prize-winner whose home was at Altenberg on the Danube. This land beneath the Enns was the birthplace,

the home or the source of inspiration for many great people — artists and scientists alike. One only has to think of Mozart and Beethoven in Baden, of Schubert in Atzenbrugg and Hinterbrühl or of Hugo Wolf in Perchtoldsdorf. Wittgenstein, the village schoolmaster, comes to mind, so does the Maria Enzersdorf circle of poets and thinkers in the Romantic age. One remembers that Kokoschka came from Pöchlarn, Raphael Donner from the Marchfeld and Prandtauer from Sankt Pölten; one recalls the Kremser Schmidt; one thinks of two more Nobel prize-winners: Landsteiner from Baden and Bertha von Suttner at Harmannsdorf. There are many, many others, down to Wystan Hugh Auden, the poet, who settled in the Vienna Woods where Weinheber had lived before him. They are a few names representing many others, just as Leopold Figl and Julius Raab stand for the whole of Austria.

Anton Wildgans was perhaps the most Lower Austrian of poets, unfashionable today, but that might change. Folk music is undergoing a revival, too, although it was regarded as more or less extinct. Contemplating the villages and listening, one notices the aptness of Ginzkey's verses for the provincial anthem, "We sing your airs, lovely as you are, and we wish to extol you, Lower Austria." Beethoven wrote the melody. In choosing it, the Lower Austrians overcame their occasional lack of self-assurance — caught, as they are, between Viennese worldliness and the independence of other provinces — and asserted themselves, recognizing the truth of Grillparzer's simple words: "It is a good land".

Pia Maria Plechl

Lower Austria comprises 19,174 km² of which 11,459 km² is a permanent settlement area with approximately 1,474,000 inhabitants. Of these some 50,000 live in St. Pölten, the provincial capital, and some 87,500 in the rural district.

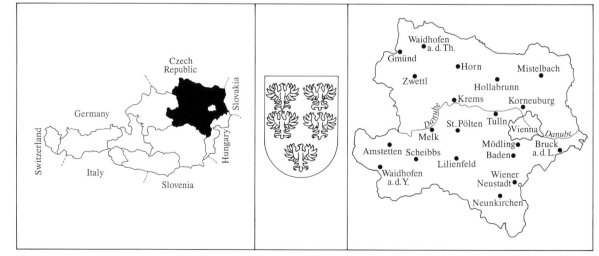

Burgenland

This is border country. The silence here has its own richness, love of life is imbued with its own drama. From behind harmless hedges generations of several thousand years have spiritedly scanned the horizon here, anxiously listening for the drone of approaching disaster. Spared the fierceness of combat and the excitement of encounter, the tranquillity of more felicitous tracts of European land is thinly monotonous and spiritually barren; the tranquillity of Burgenland is saturated with adventure. It is not the lack of events, but the profusion of life, hope and death which begets that suspended state, that balanced equilibrium.

At that spot where the Alpine chain reaches its easternmost point, breaking off the mountains, filling the valleys with scree, forming hilltops, covering the mud of a primeval sea with rubble, there was throughout the milleniums a crucible of peoples and cultures. Asiatic influences penetrated westwards across the area, European emphasis swept forcefully towards the eastern expanses. "Riding, riding, riding, through the day, through the night, through the day. / There are no more mountains, hardly a tree. Nothing dares to rise up. / Nowhere a tower. And always the same scene. One has two eyes too many. / The company lies across the Raab." The spirit of cavalry units like these is captured accurately in Rilke's "Cornet". Rarely the objective of warfare, Burgenland was again and again a marshalling area, a place for rest and readiness. Where soldiers are encamped, life is terrible and exuberant.

Having crossed the Danube basin in search of pasture land, the nomads of Asia halted here. They gazed upon considerable heights. Scouts, sent ahead, told of rocky, impassable terrain. Further west, the peaks were capped with snow, the bleak highlands could not feed the half-wild herds of cattle. The spearhead rode on, guided by the horizon behind which the sun was setting. They struggled on: to St. Gallen, to Milan, to the Rhine. But the real breakthrough failed, the mass of people left behind were still encamped east of the Alps.

Fortresses of stone, iron gateways, knights and foot-soldiers in iron armour barred the way. Earthworks, barricades, settlements of wood and clay were overrun by the storming throng of riders. What was inflammable could be conquered. Castles, mountains, weapons of steel, unwieldy orders of battle, resembling fortresses — for the nomads these had their own incomprehensible laws. They remained unintelligible for the demons of Asia. Shamanism foundered over the firmly established order of a different culture. Yet this did not remain untouched by the powers of barbaric passion and melancholy. Anyone who has ever experienced real festivities in Burgenland will have comprehended these messages from submerged cultures.

The vineyards of Burgenland grow on fertile ground, soil which covers old cultures, layer for layer. They perished here, the Scythians, Sarmatians, Alans, Pechenegs, Avars and all those others of whose names we are not even aware today. Only the tribal band which made its appearance in the ninth century succeeded in establishing a permanent state. Until the Treaty of Saint-Germain-en-Lay of 10th September, 1919 the Lower Alps remained Hungarian territory. The formal agreement was followed by a period of disorder. Not until 1921 did the representatives of the Hungarian Government undertake duly to surrender the territory of Austria.

Compared with the clash of armour and the sombre machinations of east-west activity, the north-south movement was without drama. Life on the old trading route along the edge of the Alps, connecting the North Sea and the Adriatic, remained carefully ordered even in times of war. Profitable trade avoids clamour and tries to shield its foodholds from passion and force of arms. From time immemorial the amber of the north had been exchanged for the fine wares of the Mediterranean on this route. Celts and Illyrians played a profitable part in this trade; their lively instincts still survived in our century in the alert smugglers of the period between the Wars. The "amber road" brought together the Goths of the North and

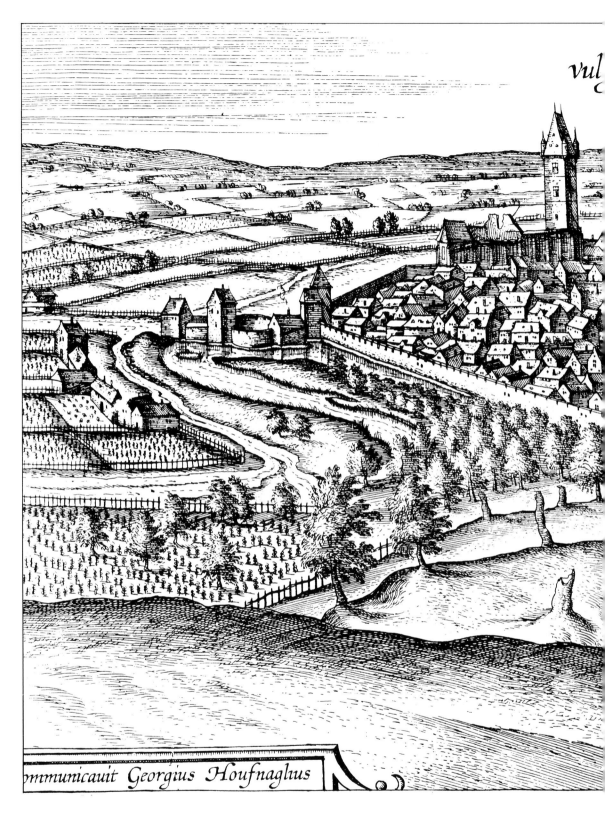

vul
c

ommunicauit *Georgius Houfnaglius*

the peoples of Greek antiquity. The mixture
became still more adventurous, the counter-
balance between the various ethnic elements
still more invigorating. The genetic chain
knows no interruption; anyone visiting Burgenland today can see them face to face, those
descendants of the peoples of North and South

who once, loaded with semi-precious stones
or with artistically fashioned weapons, met
each other here.
Products of pre-Roman life can be found in
great number in the museums at Eisenstadt
and across the border at Sopron/Ödenburg.
The archaic spirit lives on, too. The attitude

EISENSTADIVM

SNSTAT, *in vltimis finibus Auſtrię Inferioris ciuitas.*

to time is different from that of busy Central Europe with its trappings of industry. For the nomads of Asia, time was not a line, not a tangent of progress, striving after the day of the Last Judgement or — a secularized notion of the same event — after an ideal society. Time rested in itself. The cyclic recurrence of what was already familiar provided its rhythm. *Múlatni* is what the Hungarians still say when they think of holding a real celebration, *múlatni* means to let pass, signifying: to let time pass without thinking of work, of commitments, achievements, the necessities of a livelihood, but rather indulging in Dionysian

Eisenstadt, copper engraving by Georg Hufnagel, from Braun and Hogenberg's "Städtebuch", 1617.

excess, sinking into reverie, aroused and at the same time protected by the powers of Eros. An indifference towards the wish to achieve as much as possible as quickly as possible, that is what is expressed in Hungary by the verb *múlatni,* further east and south by the Russian *sitschass,* the Turkish *inschallah* and the Egyptian *schwaje.* It is familiar to the people of Burgenland, too. In it lies a force, a suspended energy, acting at the right moment.

The reasons for this composure, which springs not from equanimity, but from an experience of history, become apparent to the visitor in the village of Burg, for instance. The settlement is situated on a hill, overlooking an S-shaped loop in the Pinka river. On the right of the main road the path leads up to a modest church, set upon the plateau of the former keep. This is blocked up, covered by earth, overgrown with grass. Beneath the surface all the other living quarters are hidden, the storehouses, stalwart bastions and mighty walls of that sunken fortress. One crosses a hollow and thus passes the moat; one sits in the garden of a house at a higher level and is, in fact, above the ramparts; one walks along a deep defile and is strolling between the retaining walls of long collapsed casemates. In the front gardens ducks quack, cocks crow sleepily, old women in dark clothing turn thin faces to the sun. What do they care about the clash of weapons, silent now, in all those castles which, ever since the Hallstatt era, were erected and destroyed, erected again and destroyed again, on this spot? The population today is free from memories of the past. The machinations of the mighty, made vivid by television, arouse no more than quiet amazement. The village has witnessed too many struggles, all of them meaningless for the peasants of Burg. So why not gaze at the shadows as they slowly move eastwards and why not listen to the buzzing of the insects?

The European West made a powerfully organized appearance on two occasions in this old border country, bringing firm ideals, a hierarchical order and a fresh intermingling. The Imperium Romanum and the Holy Roman Empire gave new forms to life. They shaped the land so lastingly that all the devastation of the Turkish wars could not destroy the structure of what had been attained. The memory of a Roman heritage made a concept of the name Pannonia. It expresses the yearning for a gently creative, well ordered culture and it implies an awareness of possessing an immediate link with classical antiquity and, hence, the right to a civilized, joyful and yet spiritual way of life. But more of that later.

Like all wise imperialism, the Roman variety was primarily concerned with strengthening the Empire militarily and economically, not with suppressing or even annihilating the indigenous population. Unlike in Britain or on the Lower Rhine, the legions were spared armed combat with militant barbarians. The inhabitants of the new province of Pannonia were not savages; the proximity of the Empire had long since come to their notice. A new road network, considerable investments and efficient administration ensured that Romanization was quick and silent; trade flourished in the garrison towns; amusement quarters grew up; people soon became accustomed to the clarity of the lex romana, to the newcomers from Lusitania, Numidia, Belgica and Palestine, to the amenities of the baths and the theatres, and to the new cults. The religion of the Empire was obligatory for all freemen, but the adherents of Mithras and the Greek mysteries were no more persecuted than were the Hebrews, holding fast to their invisible God. The new military frontier lay far to the north and, eastwards, on the Danube; skirmishes along the *limes* meant good business for the war suppliers behind the lines, at times improving the general affluence; Germanic hordes who had succeeded in breaking through were soon exhausted and assimilated. Outside the towns of Scarabantia (Sopron/Ödenburg) and Savaria (Szombathely/Steinamanger) retired legionaries built their properties and villas amidst fertile estates; fruitful orchards grew up; the people savoured dates and olives, admiring camels and elephants in the circus, wearing sandals with soles of cork, collecting coins of lasting value, drinking the wine of the Mediterranean. In order to safeguard Roman exports wine growing was forbidden until the reign of Emperor Probus (AD 276—282).

At around the same time as the first vineyards were being laid out, a new religious community was attracting attention on account of its decency and its readiness for martyrdom. In the year 378 Bishop Quirinus was put to death by drowning in Scarabantia. It was the year in which the united forces of the Goths and Alans broke through the *limes.* Centuries of unrest followed, Germans and Asiatics ruled over a

The Kalvarienberg
(Mount Calvary), an
artificially formed hill
(1701 to 1707) commis-
sioned by Prince Paul
Esterházy and created by
Felix Nierinck, a Franciscan friar. Joseph Haydn
found his last resting
place in this church.

69

Oriel on Eisenstadt town hall (1650) with the municipal coat of arms. The frescos were restored in 1949 in the original early Renaissance style.

Page 71: Schloss Esterházy. Originally a medieval moated castle, it was rebuilt according to Carlo M. Carlone's design in 1663 to 1672 as a residence for the Esterházy family.

a, b) In front of the
"Heimathaus" in
Mörbisch.
c) Croatian peasant
woman in Oslip.
d) The many nesting
storks have become a
symbol of Rust.
e) Idyllic lane in
Breitenbrunn.

a) Vineyards characterize
the scenery to the west of
the Neusiedler See.
b) Farmhouse door in
Breitenbrunn.
c) The famous wine-
growing village of Oggau,
a settlement area since
the neolithic period.

a

b

c

a, c) Winter on the Neu-
siedler See at Illmitz:
The Neusiedler See is a
steppe lake with an ave-
rage depth of only one to
one and a half metres
and a wide belt of
rushes.
b) The most outstanding
medieval frescos in Bur-
genland were only disco-
vered after 1938 in the
Fischerkirche at Rust.

a

b

a) Since 1959 the quarry
at St. Margarethen has
been the scene of the
"Symposium of European
Sculptors", their creations
remain in this open-air
studio.
b) Swinging the flag in
Neckenmarkt is one of
the most interesting cus-
toms upheld in Bur-
genland.
c) Once a major border
fortress in the east,
Forchtenstein remained
uncaptured during the
Turkish Wars.

78

c

The symbol of the spa of
Bad Tatzmannsdorf.

population attempting to survive in the Roman way and, in part, in the Christian faith in half-ruined cities and devasted villages. Rome's culture was familiar to the new lords, too: often enough they had fought alongside the legions against other barbaric tribes, often enough they had exchanged messages and bartered goods. Theodoric (AD 454—526) is the best known, although not the only, example for the demeanour and education of the warrior elite. The residence of his father, Thiudimir, the Ostrogoth king, was situated in the Burgenland of today, near the Neusiedler See. Theodoric was brought up at the Byzantine court. His later law works bear witness to a superior culture, wise arbitration its aim. After the death of his father, Theodoric was proclaimed King of the Ostrogoths at the age of twenty-one. As the ally of Zeno, the Byzantine Emperor, he marched on the army of Odoacer, the Scirian, in Italy, defeating him in 493 at Ravenna. Elated by victory, the king reverted for an instant to the idols and demons of the Gothic myth. A return to the archaic: that old nomadic idea that the enemies whom they killed with their own hands would have to serve them in the other world. Theodoric slaughtered Odoacer. After the ritual murder the king ruled Italy peacefully and righteously for three decades. The sensitive balance that he achieved between the Goths and the indigenous population was not disturbed until his final years. His coins show him as a well-groomed, somewhat effeminate man, his hair carefully arranged, his expression sceptical. Germanic legend liked to see him as the valiant warrior and called him Dietrich of Bern.

Two hundred years after Theodoric's death the area again became the dominion of the European West. The first cultural encounters between man and man, tribe and tribe, were again peaceful, that is to say, they were not chronicled. The Avars who ruled the country in the eighth century maintained constant connections with the population of the south German area. Small wonder that the prospects of free property drew Bavarian and Frankish peasants eastwards. Duke Tassilo, an unfathomable and hesitant ruler, apparently did nothing to stop this migration. With his deposition by Charlemagne in 788, the area became the political interest of the Frankish Kingdom. The warrior emperor was willing to learn, forming his court at Aachen after the Byzantine example and procuring for himself the necessary legitimacy as successor of the Western Roman emperors. His espousal of Roman Catholicism filled the semblance with essence. He successfully defeated the Avars in 791; five years later Pippin, his son, forced them into subjection. Some of the nomads fled eastwards, returning to the Hungarian warband one hundred years later, others were settled in the northern Burgenland of today. Avar burial grounds have been excavated at Edelstal, Zillingtal and Leithaprodersdorf. Everything else took place — and in this respect, too, Charlemagne was an excellent pupil of Rome — according to the uniform pattern of imperial administration. An Avar march was established, the court-appointed margrave being invested with extensive rights; the Church took the lion's share of colonization: the bishoprics of Salzburg, Passau, Regensburg and Freising and the monasteries of Nieder-Altaich, St. Emmeran, Mattsee, St. Peter and Kremsmünster acquired landed property. It was now that Bavarian and Frankish peasants settled the country on a large scale. They not only found Germans, who had established themselves here a generation before them, but also a network of roads from the days of the Imperium Romanum, as well as Christian communities from the Roman era, a population of romanized Celts, Scythians, Syrians, Hebrews, Africans and Avars (not to mention all the other tribes) and, in particular, fertile arable land which could be extended by clearing. Not until the end of the ninth century did they realize that this was ancient border country. Four generations of German colonists lived peaceably. Then, in around 900, the occupation of Pannonia by the Hungarians was concluded.

The picture of that tribal band which subjugated the Lower Alps within a few decades is only hazy. The Hungarians had been on the move for centuries, mingling with other peoples west of the Urals, on the Crimea and in what today is southern Russia; their Finno-Ugrian language acquired Turkish and Old Slavonic elements; Iazygians, Kabars and Avars had moved westwards together with the leading tribes. Their leaders were no savage tribal chieftains, but men who had many links with Byzantium and with the Western Roman Empire. Shamanism, their faith, had permeated, too, due to the activities of Christian missionaries and elements of faith from the Mediterranean. The ornately decorated golden vessels of the princes show the influence of Mesopotamian craftsmen. Hittite, Iranian and Kushan influences can also be presumed. The period during which these nomads succeeded in saving themselves from downfall and adapting to the order of the European West was astonishingly brief: this, too, endorses the supposition that the quiddities of the European mind had long been familiar to the ruling class. In 907 the nomads defeated the Bavarians at Bratislava (Pressburg/Pozsony), only fifty years later they themselves were decisively defeated at the Lechfeld in Upper Bavaria by the army of Christian knighthood. Barely fifty years more were required to convince Prince Vajk of his need to be christened. Under the name Stephen, he received the royal crown from Pope Sylvester in the year 1000. He was followed by the majority of his people; the minority was forcibly converted. In the new Carolingian-style Kingdom of Hungary some of the basic Asiatic rights of free men were, however retained. Among his free lords the King was merely *primus inter pares,* the first among equals. The *gyepü* system of border defence also demanded the readiness of free men. *Gyepü* was the Hungarian name for the impassable strip of land, some fifty kilometres wide, along the border. The primeval forests were made impassable by felling trees, the wells were filled in, the swamps and wetlands were left in their original wild state and the few trading routes were secured by fortifications. As in the village of Burg, use was frequently made of old installations. Half of present-day Burgenland was *gyepü* at that time. Peasants were settled on the Hungarian side of the wilderness to defend the territory and by degrees they were elevated to the nobility as a mark of their success. The place names, Oberwart, Unterwart, Siget (= island) in der Wart, Oberschützen and Unterschützen all serve as reminders of the Kingdom's frontier guards, so do the names of the Hungarian towns, Vasvár (= iron fortress) and Sárvár (= earthwork).

Membership of the nobility was marked by various freedoms. These were there to be turned to account and vaunted in everyday life. When means were modest, the noble could set himself apart from the peasants by exhibiting his contempt for worldly goods. The paradox gave rise to a self-assurance, a sense of style. A man who is wont to carouse excessively, who with self-confident pride falls prey to the ritual of extravagance, who seeks comfort from imagined suffering in outbreaks of exaggerated sensual pleasures, is still somewhat scornfully called a *magyarone* in Burgenland today. The probe bores down through the layers of Roman-Christian culture to the domain of the nomads.

Relics of this kind do not, of course, forge a firm structure. The conversion to Christianity instigated the spiritual metamorphosis of the Hungarians. In the east of the kingdom, on the other side of the Theiss, however, the change was less thorough than here in the west. The economic consequences of the Turkish Wars meant that these archaic forms of life, long vanished even by the sixteenth and seventeenth century, were resurrected again. But the Lower Alps were spared any lasting Turkish occupation. Upon strong, never utterly destroyed, Roman foundations the old Mediterranean cultures were still at work in the spirit of a Christianity which had been active since the fourth century. Its ethos was superior to chaos. The forces of moderation and civilized accord had a normative effect. Silently and with dignity, an active patriciate shaped the urban order; artists were attracted to the nobles' castles which contained extensive libraries and which carefully cultivated a style of their own. In the sixteenth century Johannes Manlius of Württemberg was already travelling from castle to castle with his mobile printing office. He was a newspaper publisher and printer in one. His "Newe Zeitung ausz Ungern" (New Hungarian Journal) was published in 1587 in the moated castle of Eberau. Two hundred years later the castle had become a centre of freemasonry.

Under the protection of the magnates, Jewish communities flourished. Their erudition was much extolled abroad, too. An echo of this spirit can still be heard in James Joyce's *Ulysses:* his character, Leopold Bloom, comes from this area.

Croats, some of them fleeing from the Turks, others settlers of depopulated villages, brought additional colour to the culture. Their dialects gradually combined to form the Burgenlandish-Croatian literary language. This was, as it were, codified at around the turn of the century in Frankenau, a Roman settlement, by the poetry of Mathe Mersić Miloradić, the priest.

The mixture of Roman-Christian traditions, European example and original forms resulted in a peasant architecture that combined practical objectives with a sense of vigorous fullness and graceful harmony. The columns and the arcades show an assured sense of proportion. A great number of houses in the peasant baroque and peasant Classical Revival style can still be found today. The dimensions of utilitarian buildings also display an urge for architectonic solutions as part of an original, joyful aestheticism.

The notion, sometimes a strong feeling, that in all these different tendencies and works there was something unique, some link, demanded linguistic expression. The term had already been found in the fifteenth century, fading temporarily and then becoming familiar again during the long peace of Maria Theresa's epoch. Transfigured by Romanticism, "Pannonia" is still an idea that is rationally hard to define, but emotionally very moving. It appeals above all to the emotions, but it would be wrong to dismiss it as a sort of *fata morgana* of historic self-deception. It mirrors reality.

Janus Pannonius was the *nom de plume* taken by the learned Bishop of Pécs (Fünfkirchen), Janos von Csezmicze (1434—1472), the poet and humanist. This reference to the name of the former Roman province accorded with the fashion of the times, but it was also a reversion to half-buried memories. A portrait by Mantegna shows Janus Pannonius as a young, thoughtful intellectual. The reference in name and work to the old organic link with Latinity is not free from that desperate pride which Sigmund Freud's demonology calls overcompensation. Since then the term Pannonia has intruded into the language again and again, defining a geographical unit or expressing an attitude of mind that strives for tranquil balance. The centuries of war with the Turks left no time to seek a precise definition for the word; in the heat of battle terms like "the Occident" or "the Christian world" seemed more significant than the Roman appellation for an economically unimportant area, half spared by the Turks. After the great confrontation the more thoughtful souls sought their cultural identity between the foothills of the Alps and the Danube. Pannonia arose as a

shining ideal from the collected material of self-examination.

As so often, the term acquired a life of its own, reflecting a life-style which committed those people who were, or who wished to be, Pannonians. The others, too, the non-Pannonians in the surroundings, gradually became used to regarding the frame of mind in the Pannonian hills as something special, something subtle. The dream of a once-and-future Arcadia found its crystallization.

Pannonia: the very word conjures up to the eye rustic castles in which one dines temperately, in a cultivated manner, thoughtfully tasting the wine from superb cellars; conversation focuses on the verse of those poets who are anew proclaiming the harmony of creation in vigorous language; amiable erotic entanglements sometimes become tragicomedies, never catastrophes; long walks lead out of the sheltered atmosphere of well-tended grounds to nature and to the teeming richness of a village tavern in which the visitor is hit by the vitality of his own suppressed dreams; during the long winters the time is passed in sleigh rides, reading melancholy novels and holding modest musical festivities or balls: gorgeously gowned, the ladies trip along, unused to their dainty slippers, perfumed, revealing flawless skin and soft curves beneath a delicate coat of powder, and in the intervals the guests delight in a Viennese-style buffet, whilst the spirited musicians, ravenous from playing, devour the garlic sausages set before them; in the magic spring dusk the next bathing holiday is planned, so necessary for reasons of health, whilst the imagination — vacillating between a zest for life and a longing for death beneath immortal plane trees, their leaves slowly fluttering to the ground — is already conjuring up the early autumn evenings, the neighbouring landowner's habitual evening announcement that he will take his own life in the coming night on account of an unspecified disease. And because all this is so important, the mighty and their vassals throughout the land are little heeded; the rulers come and go; they are far distant; a crisply fried black pudding holds more significance than the political constellations. Pannonia means recognition of the transience and thus, in the long view, the ineffectiveness of government. Pannonia means the validity of poetry by way of vitality and, at the same time, the transfiguration of joy by way of poetry. People who do not comprehend the euphoria of the senses or the metaphysics of the dreaming soul remain strangers. The gentle law of balance tolerates neither prodigality nor puritanism.

After Burgenland finally became a part of Austria, it sank into leisurely repose. The latent social conflicts did, however, produce a tense atmosphere. Here, too, this led to confrontation between the Social Democrats and the Christian Socialists. On 15th July, 1927 enmity reached a pitch: regarding a Social Democrat parade as a threat, some Christian Socialists in the village of Schattendorf took up their rifles and fired into the crowd, killing a child and an invalid. The subsequent trial in Vienna ended with the acquittal of the accused. Embittered crowds protested against the verdict, setting alight the Palace of Justice; the police intervened and there were numerous deaths. Retrospectively, the incident seems to have signified the onset of the brief and bloody civil war of 1934. Those to benefit from Austria's internal strife were the National Socialists. After Hitler annexed the country in 1938, incorporating it in his Third Reich, Burgenland was dissolved as a separate Federal Province and was divided up between Lower Austria (called Lower Danube at that time) and Styria. Not until 1945 did the country acquire its former sovereignty. With the departure of the occupation forces ten years later, conditions prevailed for a gradual upward swing.

Since then the outward appearance of the province has changed in many ways. With the departure of poverty, the unprepossessing examples of an anonymous architecture were replaced by comfortable, new houses; a new road network brought the remotest villages in touch with the achievements of technical civilization and dislodged the customs of archaic life; new tourist facilities benefited local people and visitors alike, but did alter the traditional appearance of the villages and the scenery here and there. The richly stratified culture and the urge for equilibrium remained unchanged.

In the ancient border country they are used to the constantly changing surface. A temporary halt neither gives rise to a hope for eternal peace, nor to the fear that, detached from world history, the place might again sink into a state of permanent backwardness. The convergence of many cultures has produced an alert, cirumspect race in whom the vitality of the many bygone peoples lives on. Nothing disappears finally or without trace, every deed, every omission still has its effect down through the centuries, every word uttered, every silence has a life-forming significance for all time. In Burgenland the link between cause and effect, the emergence of life from death, the permanence in change are obvious for the listening awareness. The border country is an area of transition: not just in space, but in its feeling for time, too, the perception of a constant, usually soundless metamorphosis takes effect. It teaches that bold hopes should be examined critically, but that dreams, too, should be heeded.

György Sebestyén

Burgenland comprises 3,965 km² of which 2,578 km² is a permanent settlement area with approximately 217,000 inhabitants. Of these some ten thousand live in Eisenstadt, the provincial capital, and some 36,000 in the surroundings.

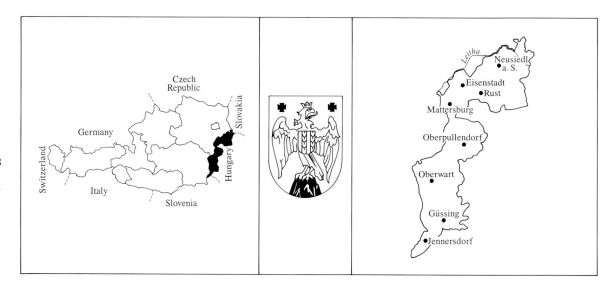

Styria

There is something special about the Styrian scenery. Craggy peaks, deeply wooded gorges, gently merging hills and spreading valleys, the dream and the lucid reality of the capital city of this province, the endless stretch of vineyards — all this is permeated with a sense of space, a promise of perfection.

Contemplating Styria's varied scenery and its multitude of shapes and forms, one is reminded perhaps of Tuscany in the early summer or of Venice in the winter, so deep is the impression left. It is difficult to define in words, but the perceptive beholder will sense it when confronted with the glacier world of the Dachstein or when driving through the Ennstal at the foot of the sheer face of the Grimming, he will sense it when tatters of morning mist float across the valley between the sombre barns or when pine forests summon the faithful like some green cathedral spire. He will sense it amidst the Salzkammergut lakes and when he gazes at those kindly mountain ridges surrounding Graz, ridges in which the might of the Alps expires; he will sense it, too, in a bright summer's meadow amongst the east Styrian hills or amidst the orchards and vineyards of western and southern Styria, when the ripe fruits and the russet woods of autumn unfurl their splendour beneath a blue sky interwoven with gold. Inexplicable enchantment, not compelling speech, yet unravelling the mystery of the place.

A study of the landscape brings one closer to the truth about the people in this region. It must be regarded as an acknowledged fact that "Nature herself did not provide for a self-contained province with distinct borders and with fixed points of order for a community of people. No invitation existed to create from seemingly divergent landscapes a uniform pattern which could acquire the character of a province. The only conclusion remaining is that Styria's becoming a province was not spontaneous, but was a gradual process, a result of conscious decisions, man's creation. Human understanding and human action perceived and grasped a central core in the midst of partial landscapes which fitted together to form a unity. 'Pushed together' by outside forces — by those 'powers of history' from which no country and no people can escape — it slowly and gradually acquired an existence and an autonomy of its own. The various contributory factors can no longer be established, but — however it happened — man 'discovered' this province, gave it form and purpose, or found a purpose in it."*

From the time when the first people settled here some hundred thousand years before the birth of Christ until the present day Styria has always had important tasks to fulfil, whether as a bulwark to ward off repeated attacks by the Hungarians, Turks and French, as the occasional imperial residence, as an important site at the beginning of industrialization in Central Europe at the time of Archduke Johann or, finally, as a cultural pivot, again making the province a focus of European interest today by way of the "Steirische Herbst" event or thanks to the reputation of its poets and its university.

The race of people who inhabit Styria and who still have to bear much of the burden of difficulties pressing upon Austria from the outside and the inside today were moulded by an eventful history. Their main role usually consisted of supporting others and fighting for others in order to survive themselves. The glittering highlights were extremely few and far between. The harshness of fate and a landscape which, despite its beauty, gives away nothing made these people what they are today: people distinguished by self-assurance and a love of liberty, people whose nature harbours an intimation of space — this is inherent in the Styrian landscape — which crystallizes in the reality of an open, friendly way of life and genuine liberality.

Numerous peoples settled for longer and shorter periods in the area which is now Styria and it was usually a component of other states chosen for purposes of defence. Illyrians, Venetians, Celts, Romans and Slavs settled here successively, leaving traces of their cul-

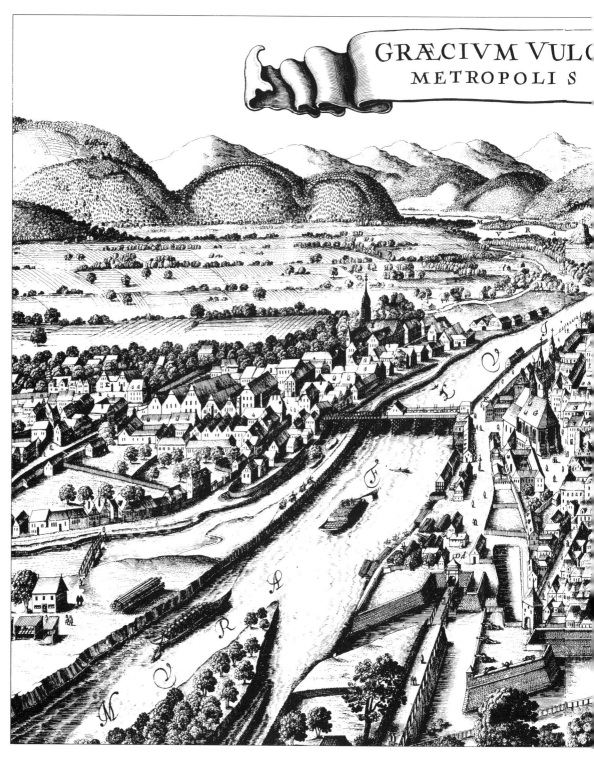

ture and of their talents. Styria was once incorporated in the kingdom of Noricum and in the Roman province of the same name, it was a part of Pannonia and, later, part of the Duchy of Carantania. It was always a border country, towards Pannonia for the people of Noricum, towards the east for the Carantanians or, in 970 as the "marcha carentana" — the first time it was so designated — intended as a protective southern flank for the northern mark of "Ostarrichi". The phrase "no Austria without Styria" first started to acquire meaning at that time and is still uttered with pride today. The course of history — during which the area became known as "Stireland", the Margraviate and, finally, the Duchy of Styria — made the burden of duties borne for Austria by the "marcha carantana" no easier.

But back to the period at the turn of the first millenium after the birth of Christ. At first the

RATZ
IÆ.

Graz, copper engraving
by Laurentius van de
Sype and Wenzel Hollar,
Jansson Germania 1657.

Eppensteins ruled Styria until this authority was transferred in 1055 to the Traungau family. One hundred and twenty five years after coming to power this line of counts succeeded in acquiring the status of an independent duchy for their border region on the river Mur and for the various marches and counties which had since become part of it.

Anxious to retain the balance of power in his empire, Frederick Barbarossa formed the opinion that the Bavarian duke was too generous with the abundant powers granted him by the emperor. He therefore excluded Styria and other areas from the duke's feudal rights. In 1180 he made his nephew, Ottokar IV, duke and placed him on a level with the Bavarian. Ottokar was a sick man, however, and was not destined to live long or to be blessed with heirs. When he died of leprosy in 1192, his line died with him and the Babenbergs became rulers of Styria in accordance with his wishes. The Georgenberg document of 1168 had secured the rights of the Styrian great vassals. Duke Leopold of Austria — Ottokar bequeathed his duchy to him — secured these rights for his successors, too, and stipulated at Georgenberg that the Styrians be allowed to appeal to the emperor and to invoke a princely court, should their ruler prove to be tyrannical. The rights or "liberties" which the Styrian nobility acquired here are to be regarded as the rights of the province itself and they underline the constitutional significance of the Georgenberg document.

On the basis of this document the Babenberg era became the great era for the Styrian noble vassals. They became the upholders of Styria's self-awareness and this was to have a decisive effect during the period of interregnum. After the death of the last Babenberg, Frederick the quarrelsome, in 1246, Styria became an object of contention between Bohemia and Hungary. When at first it was ceded to Hungary in the treaty of Ofen — this was drawn up thanks to the mediation of the Pope — the Styrian nobles successfully rebelled against Hungarian rule.

Finally, in 1260, the treaty of Vienna awarded the area to Přemysl Ottokar who had defeated Bela IV, the king of Hungary, and who gradually brought back security and peace to Styria. The regard in which this Bohemian was first held soon cooled, however, when he placed increasing pressure on the Styrian nobles. The Styrians rose up against him and joined forces with Rudolf of Habsburg. He had been elected king in 1273 and four years later, on 18th February, 1277, he confirmed the rights previously granted to the Styrian great vassals by earlier rulers and he also pledged that he would only confer the duchy of Styria on that prince in whom the majority of vassals voiced their trust.

Styria's reputation and its burden grew in proportion to the House of Austria's responsibility for the whole German Empire. While serving Austria, the province stood the test and was consolidated. "Its capital increasingly became a meeting-point for intellectual, cultural, economic and political forces. It was thus a natural consequence that Styria should become the 'Vorland' of all inner Austrian territories from the Alps to the Adriatic when this

Bruck an der Mur, copper engraving by G. M. Vischer, Topographia Ducatus Stirae 1681.

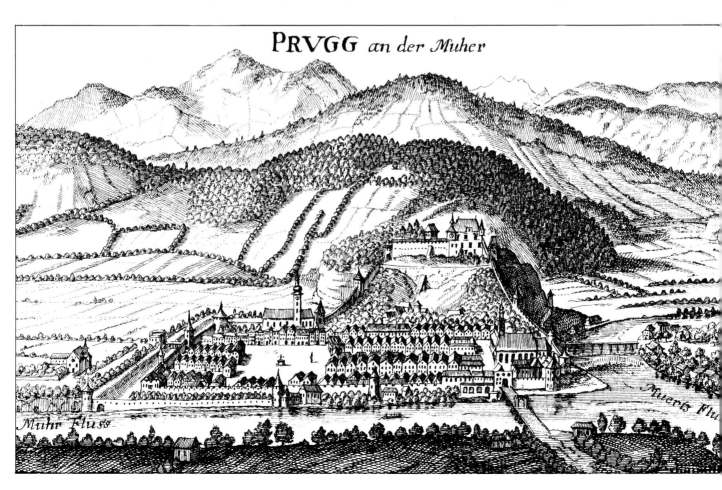

PRVGG an der Muher

Page 90/91:
The might and majesty of the southern flank of the Dachstein, looking towards the Ennstal.

On the Styrian iron road:
a) The Erzberg between
Eisenerz and Vordernberg
was worked even in
Roman days and gave
Styria the name "the iron
mark".
b) The wrought-iron
fountain casing in Vor-
dernberg and the "Korn-
messerhaus" (c) in Bruck
an der Mur (1499 to
1505) bear witness to
medieval affluence.

Page 94/95: The "Flin-
serl" carnival on Shrove
Tuesday in Bad Aussee
(b) and the Samson
pageant (a) after the St.
Oswald's procession (c)
in Krakaudorf are exam-
ples of the wide variety
of Styrian customs.
d) The narcissus fields in
the Ausseerland are as
well-known as the Aussee
Narcissus Festival.
e) The Toplitzsee in the
Styrian Salzkammergut.

d

e

95

a) Late autumn on the Styrian wine route.
b, c) In the vineyards of southern Styria.

Page 98:
The Herrengasse front and the arcaded courtyard of the Landhaus in Graz, seat of the Styrian Provincial Government. Lavishly redesigned in 1557 by Domenico dell'Allio, the Italian architect, the Landhaus is one of the most outstanding Renaissance buildings in Austria.

Page 99:
View of the old town, the Cathedral and the Mausoleum from Graz Schloßberg with its characteristic clock tower.

A detail of the fountain in Graz Stadtpark, designed by J. J. Klagenauer for the 1873 World Exhibition in Vienna and later erected in Graz.

inner Austria was institutionalized as an independent state in 1564; Graz, as the ruling prince's residence, became the capital of inner Austria. It constituted the main stronghold against the Turks in the great line of defence to the south-east which was administered by Styria's ruler as incumbent of the eternal and perpetual generalship of the Slovene and Croatian borders. Graz was also the capital where the religious struggle was waged most fiercely, it was moreover the city of learning and of scholars who went about their work at the Jesuit University founded by Archduke Karl II and at the evangelical school foundation which was maintained by the Styrian estates. Despite the fact that he was a Protestant, Johannes Kepler nevertheless maintained professorial connections with colleagues at the Catholic university. These were turbulent, sorrowful and great times for Graz and for Styria. The province had recognized its dimensions and the efforts which originated here for peaceful coexistence between German, Slovene and Latin peoples are still reflected in the outward countenance of the city today."*

Not only in its outward appearance either: the annual "Steirischer Herbst" event provides an intellectual and artistic meeting-point for Italy, Slovenia and Austria in Graz, an obvious indication of how Inner Austria's intellectual range has remained durable up to the present day.

But let us return to those days when, as a belated consequence of the "Styrian" Emperor Ferdinand's moving his residence to Vienna in 1749, Graz lost its pre-eminence as the capital of Inner Austria. The splendour held so dear finally began to pale and this region which over the centuries had suffered more than its share of disasters and which had been menaced by Hungarians, Turks, the plague, locusts, French troops and economic distress was once more hit by hard times. Once again the area was pushed away into a corner of history and it was in a most lamentable condition when, almost miraculously and just at the right moment, Archduke Johann of Austria arrived in languishing Styria — his royal brother had forbidden him to remain in his beloved Tyrol — to become its great saviour as "Styrian prince".

Mariazell, copper engraving by G. M. Vischer, Topographia Ducatus Stirae 1681.

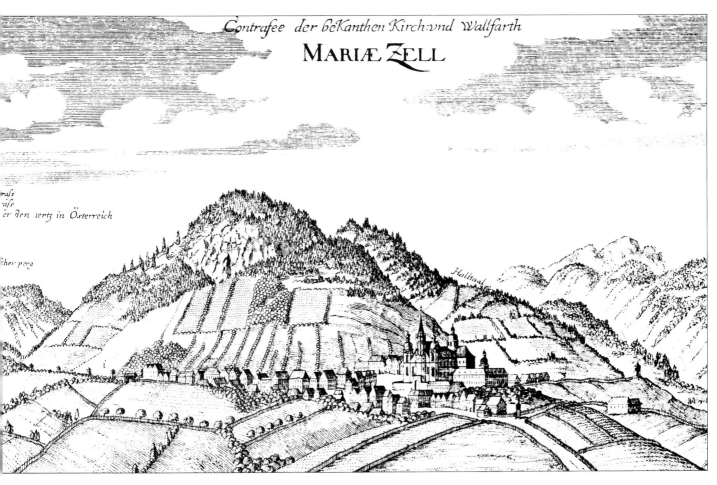

Contrafée der bekanthen Kirch-vnd Wallfarth

MARIÆ ZELL

Here mention must be made of the part played by the Church in the province's development. Long before Styria or even a duchy had come into being, the various religious orders had shaped the land spiritually, this having a decisive influence on the way it took shape materially. The members of these orders built the churches, new centres of spiritual life, they started to establish great libraries, they pioneered schooling and they sent out their priests to the remotest borders of solitude and to the far-scattered settlements of the land in order to preach the gospel.

The influence of the monasteries was in truth immeasurable, embracing the nobles in their castles and palaces and their servants below stairs, colouring their attitudes and their actions. Thus upon his arrival here Archduke Johann encountered people who were prepared to accept him and his ideas, enabling him to set about creating his Utopia and together with them to lead the province away from poverty and backwardness to become a flourishing community.

Whether fighting hunger and pestilence, find-

ing new and better methods for agriculture and forestry — and for the industry which was just emerging at that time — nurturing science by founding the Joanneum, the university in Graz or the school of mining in Leoben, providing new means of communication for Styria, such as the southern railway line, or opening up foreign markets for Styrian products, Archduke Johann found willing helpers and open-minded people, ready to understand him and prepared to carry out his work with him for Styria. The benefits of much of it can still be felt in our day. Nevertheless, Styria has been spared little since Archduke Johann's time. After the First World War it lost one third of its territory in the south and the Second World War, too, left its traces. Bombing, the fact that the province was at times part of the scene of fighting, and the occupation after the War all took their toll. But Styria has throughout the course of its history always remained true to its task as a border province in south-east Austria and the German-speaking area, a task it has admirably fulfilled.

It continues to do so today by remaining on

Leoben, copper engraving by G. M. Vischer, Topographia Ducatus Stirae 1681.

DER PASS SCHADWIENN VND VÖSTVNG CLAM VON DER STEYRMARCKHT HER AN ZVSEHEN

Warten ſtain

The Schottwien Pass and Klamm Fortress, seen from Styria, copper engraving by G. M. Vischer, Topographia Archiducatus Austriae Inf. 1672.

good terms with its neighbours and by helping to ensure that the border is more and more a "quickset hedge" across which people are only too pleased to join hands. Centuries of defending their rights have formed the people of Styria, giving them a natural self-assurance and making them able and willing to recognize a compromise and to act accordingly.

Thanks to its inhabitants' industry and their artistic strain, Styria has always succeeded in wresting the necessities of life from Nature and in developing a high standard of culture in the domestic, professional and artistic spheres. The people's candour and their talent for moderation have obviously served them to good purpose here.

The natural resources upon which the Styrian economy was based from the very beginning were prolific forest, iron and coal. Iron ore, silver and magnesium carbonate were the basic elements of industrialization. In order to smelt the ore a better source of energy than wood was soon required; coal mining thus developed. An army of hard-working farmers

looked after everyone, ensuring that the table was stocked with every necessity.

It would be self-deception not to recognize that this very structure of the Styrian economy was the root of those difficulties which it is experiencing today. Survival can only be secured by an imaginative process of re-thought. The number of self-employed far-mers has dropped to eight per cent of the total population. Sixty per cent of Styria is wooded land and developments on the international timber market mean that economic problems are encountered here, too. International struc-tural changes have aggravated the situation on the iron and steel sector.

Styria is making every effort to deal with these developments. New ideas are being applied to adapt industry to high-quality products; tou-rism is an ever-growing sector and capitalizes on agriculture without depleting it. Styria's natural assets are being supplemented by amenities like thermal baths, artifical bathing lakes, indoor swimming pools, ski lifts, paths, golf courses and riding stables. These, together with the warm hospitality encountered in Styrian family establishments, constitute a major attraction for visitors from Austria and abroad.

As tireless cultivators of the scenery, the farmers, whose role is grossly underestimated, ensure that this important asset is tended and cherished. Their work helps to ensure that the landscape is conserved in its full beauty for posterity. Now, on the threshold of the second industrial age, Styria is a sound blend of well-tended, vital scenery and an expandable and adaptable economy. Even if the latter is not free from problems, it can nevertheless face the future optimistically, backed by the knowledge and expertise of Styrian educational establishments and supported by the Styrian people's patience and industry.

Those in search of art's legacy to the province and wishing to become acquainted with the Styrian gifts and abilities will set out from the monasteries and churches, the castles and palaces, and will proceed to the chapels and wayside crucifixes and to those examples of modern secular art to be found in museums and in the architecture.

Outstanding examples here are the minsters of Neuberg, Seckau, St. Lambrecht, Rein, Admont and Vorau with their art treasures and their libraries, then St. John's chapel at Pürgg, the pilgrimage churches of Mariazell and Maria Strassengel, the Landhaus, the castle, the cathedral and Ferdinand II's mausoleum in Graz and, as one example of the many palaces and castles throughout the province, Eggenberg castle, not to mention countless other churches, great houses and monuments.

The artists and scientists who helped to shape this province are legion: Pietro de Pomis and Pietro Valnegro, the builders of the mausoleum in Graz, Johann Bernhard Fischer von Erlach, that genius who designed its interior, Joseph Thaddäus Stammel and Veit Königer, the sculptors, Johann Joseph Fux and Hugo Wolf, the composers, Robert Hamerling, Peter Rosegger, Max Mell, Paula Grogger and Franz Nabl, the poets, or Fritz Pregl, Julius Wagner-Jauregg, Erwin Schrödinger, Otto Loewi and Karl von Frisch, the Nobel prize-winners, all enhanced Styria's reputation, shaping its atmosphere of intellectual enlightenment. Thanks to their contribution, Styria has become a home of young art, its broad spectrum embracing events like the "Forum Stadtpark" and the "Steirischer Herbst", a uniquely comprehensive avant-garde festival in which conservative artists also take their regular place. Avant-garde music and plays are just as much a part of the theatre scene here as are the works of Richard Wagner, Mozart, Verdi, Richard Strauss, Goethe, Shakespeare, Anouilh and Nestroy.

A glance at the list of artists who have worked and still work in Styria shows how very varied are the movements represented. All — painters, sculptors, composers, musicians, poets and writers — have found here that free environment which makes their creativity possible.

Its nature and its uniqueness make Styria a place where great things are possible and have been achieved. Equally, it is a place where small things have their justification, interwoven in the tapestry of history, suspended in a landscape which gives an intimation of perfection.

* The quotations are taken from an essay by Landtagspräsident Prof. Dr. Hanns Koren.

Johannes Koren

Styria comprises 16,388 km² of which 5,165 km² is a permanent settlement area with approximately 1,185,000 inhabitants. Of these some 238,000 live in Graz, the provincial capital, and some 118,000 in the surroundings.

Upper Austria

When someone has to write about Upper Austria, when he was born in this area and when he lives there, problems arise.

Various attitudes are possible, of course. One can take shelter behind erudition, thus creating a platform for self-criticism, for self-publicity, for philosophical analysis. Be that as it may, the final result will be subjective and, for the sake of truth, it will have to remain subjective.

When the person having to write about Upper Austria also happens to be a dramatist, won't he perhaps be tempted to emphasize for effect? The Hallstatt culture, the Peasants' Wars, the scenic contrasts between north and south, the arts as represented by Bruckner, Stifter and Kubin, the pugnacity of the Innviertel people, the province's industrial wealth, the Mühlviertel jokes . . .?

He will. Definitely.

Above all, however, he will make plain the relationship between landscape and people, between history and character, and he will firmly resist the temptation to dominate the scene himself.

Of the Austrian provinces Upper Austria is without doubt — and I say this deliberately — one of the most attractive. But the problem is of a different nature: whilst perhaps the Tyrol is regarded as the mountain province, Vienna as the cultural centre or charm metropolis, Carinthia as the lake district, Vorarlberg as the Austrian Switzerland and Styria as green, there is no image which aptly defines the area above the Enns.

Suddenly confronted with the question, "What does Upper Austria mean to you?", many would be hard put to find a prompt reply. So would I.

To avoid getting on the wrong track: Upper Austria has many friends, many who hold it dear, people who bring their case with eloquence and fervour, it just all depends on which part of the province they favour. There are many who have for years been spending the summer in the Salzkammergut and who do so again and again, many whose loyalty to the Mühlviertel is equally intense, many who are capitivated by the austerely rugged scenery of the Eisenwurzen beyond Steyr and many who almost long for a useful little ailment so that they can betake themselves to one of the spas and recuperate at leisure in the rurally urbane atmosphere of the Upper Austrian towns.

Until next summer.

Until the next cure.

All the many different devotees do not get in each other's way. Those intent on mountains remain in the south, those in search of natural, unspoilt countryside have their Sauwald.

Upper Austria offers all of that. And more: castles and palaces, abbeys steeped in tradition, industrial regions, imperturbable farming land moulded generations ago, rivers, valleys and lakes, ancient customs, modern infrastructure and, still, something virgin, hidden, unheeded, kept secret, jealously guarded by connoisseurs, treasures still to be unearthed. Someone once expressed it like this: a lady whose profile isn't exactly Grecian might be admired for her charm, another for her irresistible eyes, another for her marvellous legs; Upper Austria has no need to conceal her eyes or legs, her profile and her charm are notable, but because there is no really outstanding, dominating feature one acquires the impression that she is nothing special.

In actual fact, the area between the Dachstein and the Dreisesselberg, between the Enns and the Inn contains all the characteristic Austrian landscapes in a confined space. Perhaps that is one reason for the boastfully ironic saying that the province is more than Austria — namely, Upper Austria! I have often heard that said, but have yet to meet anyone who really meant it. The people here might be self-assured, but superlatives are not a facet of their character and talking big is not their style.

The Viennese sing the praises of their Danube, but it does flow right across Upper Austria, too, and surely it is nowhere more delightful than at Vichtenstein, where it breaks through, and at Engelhartszell down to the Schlögener Schlinge.

Linz an der Donau,
copper engraving by
F. B. Werner
and J. F. Probst,
c. 1732.

At 2,995 metres, the Dachstein cannot quite compete with the mountains in the provinces of Salzburg or the Tyrol, but it is just as rugged, just as angular, just as suited to songs and legends. A few kilometres further east are the Tote Gebirge, the "dead mountains". The main peak in that range, the Grosse Priel, has even been rated as one of the loveliest mountains in the world. Not by the local people — as we said before, superlatives are not their line, but by Edward Compton, the English painter of the Alps, a man who certainly could not be accused of local patriotism. The Tote Gebirge mainly consist of Dachstein limestone, water fails to remain on the cleft surface and seeps into the crevices, collecting in underground streams and leaching out a ramified network of passages, grottoes and caves. Springs are almost completely absent on the surface; a stone desert has come into being, massively macabre, only providing living space for a few taller animals. Man has paid his contribution — and not just with his confounded chemistry — towards making the mountains even more "dead". In the eighteenth century the mountain game was completely exterminated here, poachers being to blame — poachers and a superstition according to which anyone possessing the heart bone of an ibex he himself has shot will acquire infallible marksmanship and, almost more important, will never be hit by a hunter's bullet.

The Salzkammergut is that part of the province which was opened up to tourism at an early date. The scenic beauties, the lakes, the courtesy of the people and the soothing effect of the salt water combined must have encouraged the Viennese aristocracy to endure a postchaise journey of three and a half days in order to spend their holiday here. Finally, when Ischl became as it were the summer residence of the old monarchy, the Salzkammergut area attained the higher realms of operetta.

The only pity was that, due to its similarity of name, the Salzkammergut area was frequently associated with the province of Salzburg. And still is.

Upper Austria remains unperturbed about this. The inhabitants of the province are hardly to be found at the Attersee, Traunsee and Mondsee lakes, or at Traunstein, Gmunden and St. Wolfgang; they prefer to spend their holidays somewhere in the Almtal, in the southern Innviertel, the Ibmer Moos or the Eisenwurzen districts. Of these it is sometimes claimed that it is no use expecting scenic attractions, but anyone leaving his car behind and relying on his feet, his eyes and his nose can fall in love with places ignored by the passing traveller.

The inveterate connoisseurs of such landscapes are like mushroom gatherers — loath to reveal the best spots even to their oldest friends!

There might be some people who remain unmoved by the hilly domain of the Mühlviertel, finding it boring, dull, monotonous. Adalbert Stifter occupied himself with this landscape all his life and never tired of it, but was continually discovering some new facet. "On my first visit to these highlands I noticed that it seemed more silent and more peaceful than when I journeyed through other, quiet, peaceful landscapes. I thought no more of it. Now this sensation returned. In this countryside the few places of any size are far apart, the farmsteads stand solitary on hills, in deep ravines or on unsurmised slopes. Round about are fields, meadows, groves and rock. The streams run softly in the ravines and, where they rush, their rushing is not heard because the paths very frequently run along the heights." It is simple countryside that Stifter describes, a district requiring a second glance. But perhaps that is the secret, perhaps that is why the artist approaches it with such intensity: one is nearer to the roots.

An area related to the Mühlviertel — and not just geologically — is the Sauwald at the corner of the Inn and the Danube between Schärding and Wesenufer. "That is an area one can succumb to, as one succumbs to a woman, or to drink!"

Alfred Kubin settled here as a young man and never got away. He portrayed the original, ghostly, grotesque, secretive, sinister, special, strange and strangely lovely elements of this area in hundreds of drawings and, had he lived twice, he would never have run out of themes.

The passer-by will hardly be aware that the centre of Upper Austria contains a massive industrial area. Somehow the roads succeed in skirting these deceptively and apparently enough land remains to squeeze itself in between as a buffer.

The land above the Enns has always possessed a certain economic significance. Salt — once as valuable as gold — in the Salzkammergut, brown coal in the Hausruck area, the timber industry in the Mühlviertel, iron processing by the foundries, nailsmiths and cutlers in the Ennstal. The heavy industry in Ranshofen, in Steyr and above all in Linz is only a few decades old and did not grow, but was set up more or less artificially and strategically. Due to the particular historic circumstances, Linz was not such an obvious capital as is the case in other provinces. The south was oriented towards Salzburg thanks to its vicinity and to the communications; the Innviertel belonged to Bavaria until about two hundred years ago and the Mühlviertel only gravitated so strongly towards Linz when the northern border was hermetically sealed — bygone history now — and the large concerns on the other side of the Danube provided the only means of livelihood for many.

On a balmy summer evening, when one approaches Linz by boat from Aschach, with the Pöstlingberg and its unmistakable church on the left and the old part of the city and the castle on the right, the lights mirrored in the Danube, then the city is silent and dreamy. In

Freistadt, copper engraving by Matthäus Merian, Topographia Austriae 1649.

reality and in the light of day Linz is anything but romantic.

There is an impressive main square, but in general the town threads its way to the left and right of one single road. Even its most vehement adherents would not call Linz a gem among cities. What is more, industrial emission places a particular burden on the air here. References to the good climate in Linz are meant politically, they refer to the unaggressive manner in which ideological differences are settled. The air is sometimes heavy with dust from the VOEST factory or it smells of fertilizer from the Stickstoffwerke or, according to the direction of the wind, of coffee from the Franck-Kathreiner Nestle company.

Nevertheless the ironic saying "Oh, to be in Linz" is apt: unlike the Viennese or the citizen of Salzburg, the Linzer does not grumble about his city. And he has another distinguishing feature, the Linzer: he is probably the only townsman who does not regard himself as a yardstick out in the country. On weekdays he meets people from Zwettl or Eferding as colleagues at work, or shopping in one of the numerous shops and supermarkets, and in the evening or at week-ends he meets them again, in Zwettl or in Eferding, over "Grammelknödel" and smoked bacon.

The people of Linz display no arrogance at being inhabitants of the capital. Is it because Wels was originally intended as the metropolis of this province above the Enns? Is it because, for centuries, Bavarian Passau was the religious centre of the entire area stretching well into Lower Austria? Is it because of the eccentric obstinacy of the people of the Innviertel, Mühlviertel, Traunviertel and Hausruckviertel and their reluctance to be governed centrally? Or is it simply because of the amiable charm of the people of Linz? Who can say . . .

Linz is an economically potent town, there is no doubt about that, Linz is a useful town and, with its Neue Galerie, ars electronica, Bruckner festival and Jägermayrhof literature competition, it exerts a cultural influence which is registered throughout Austria and beyond its borders.

The ironmonger Hans Brandstetter died in 1521. He owned six houses in Steyr including the municipal baths, six houses in Steyrdorf, two farms with gardens and meadows, a house in Eferding, the manor of Ramingdorf and the office of Oehling.

I do not mention this in order to show how a rich ironmonger bought up land in half of Upper Austria except Linz, I quote it because civic affluence and a certain need for prestige seem to feature in the character of these towns above the Enns.

Although their historical development did not run a parallel course, Freistadt, Enns, Schärding, Hallstatt, Steyr, Braunau and Obernberg have much in common. The houses in the town centres are closely huddled together, trying to push each other aside, to steal a bit of room with an alcove, to show off a bit more with the facade. The streets behind the attractive town squares are narrow, winding, often hardly wide enough for an ox-cart, uneven, with projecting walls, niches, irregular, as if the builders had abandoned set square and plumbline and relied on their own sense of proportion.

And, in another way, it is the sense of proportion that is so striking in these old towns. Even the richest ironmonger would never have dreamed of building a house which, in form, size, taste or height, was out of tune with the rest, thus perhaps spoiling the overall effect. (Many a modern architect would do well to exercise such a sense of proportion today, when concreting up the landscape with factories, hotels, banks and insurance monsters!)

What makes Upper Austrian towns outstanding is their sensuousness, their warmth, their humour, their love of colour and their inhabitants' apitude for combining the useful with the beautiful and the beautiful with the useful. There is much of which we no longer have precise knowledge, but every seemingly high-spirited detail, every picture, every ornament has its history and its own special meaning.

Opposite the Rathaus in the lower town square at Schärding there is a fresco depicting two men with wooden poles growing out of their eyes. The inscription runs: "Hypocrite! First remove the beam from thine eye, then shalt thou see to remove the mote from thy brother's eye."

Well-versed in the Scriptures, the people of Schärding — so one might think . . .

In fact, the picture is an act of defiance going back to a dispute between the owner of the house and the "honourable magistrate". The house owner had the painting done in revenge for unjust treatment and, to his own wrath and

The Parish Church of
Hallstatt on the south-
west bank of the Hallstät-
ter See.

The Gosausee with the Hohe Dachstein (2,995 m.) in the background.

Page 111:
a) The "Emperor's villa" in Bad Ischl, once the summer residence of Emperor Franz Joseph.
b) For centuries the Hallstatt Corpus Christi procession has been held on the lake. The richly decorated raft bearing the Blessed Sacrament is accompanied by a vessel carrying the band and by numerous small boats.

a

b

111

a) Innviertel scenery between Wels and Ried.
b—d) The joys of Krems-münster Abbey.
b) The Tassilo goblet (769).
c) The Gunther tomb.
d) Fish pool (by C. A. Carlone, enlarged by Jakob Prandtauer).

Page 114/115:
a) Detail from the central shrine of the Kefermarkt altar (1490 to 1497), one of the most famous examples of late Gothic carving work.
b) Wintry mist at Ried in the Innviertel.
c) Mühlviertel farmhouse to the south of Freistadt.
d, e) Women wearing the popular Upper Austrian festive costume at a harvest thanksgiving procession in Leopoldschlag, Mühlviertel.

a) The Stadtturm (1565 to 1568) in the centre of the main square is an Enns landmark.

b) Steyr is one of the most romantic towns in Austria. Most of the houses in the Stadtplatz date back to the late Gothic period.

c) Town square in Schärding.

b

c

a) The Bruckner organ in the Abbey of Augustinian Canons at St. Florian is one of the finest sounding examples of its age. Anton Bruckner was the organist here from 1845 to 1855.
b) The town of Linz acquired a musical and cultural centre with the Brucknerhaus, built in 1969 to 1974. It is the annual scene of the international Bruckner Festival.
c) The Pilgrimage Church (1738 to 1774, spires 1892) on the Pöstlingberg on the left bank of the Danube is a symbol of Linz.

Baroque and Biedermeier still characterize the old town of Linz; in the centre, the apothecary's house, its facade dating back to 1735.

the derision of the people of Schärding, the alderman in his chambers opposite was constantly confronted with his own likeness as a hypocrite.

But even the highest authorities were powerless in the face of art and the Bible.

A Mühlviertel man meets a man from Burgenland. The latter starts to lament: "These Viennese", he says, "they're forever telling jokes about us."

"Just like the people of Linz about us", commiserates the Mühlviertel man.

"But they buy up our houses."

"Precisely."

"They drink our wine and in the summer they come in thousands for water skiing on the Neusiedler See."

"On the Neusiedler See?"

"Yes, that large lake on the Hungarian border . . ."

"I know that", says the Mühlviertel man, "but I didn't realize it was so steep . . ."

These Mühlviertel jokes have suddenly come into circulation in recent years, they are recounted at every suitable and unsuitable opportunity and there seems to be an inexhaustible store. They are funniest, of course, when someone from the Mühlviertel district is also one of the circle.

I know sufficient people from the Mühlviertel and I find nothing about them which makes them particularly predestined to be the butt of jokes.

They are sincere, reliable people, ambitious and bluff, people who can come to grips with something, tough, like the soil in which they are rooted, thrifty, industrious . . . Whatever else they might be, they are not funny. Certainly no funnier than the inhabitants of any other area.

When God had finished creating the earth he saw that he had a heap of stones left over and he instructed his angels to put these stones in a bag and to sink them deep in the sea. But whilst the angels were flying north across the Danube, the Devil came secretly and slit open the bag with a long knife so that all the stones fell out and were scattered over the whole Mühlviertel.

And this soil along the Gusen, the Rodl and the Mühl is in truth hard and stony, making it difficult enough for the farmer to wrest a frequently meagre annual harvest. That cannot have been God's plan so, according to the legend, it must have been the Devil who was responsible for creating the Mühlviertel.

The real Upper Austrian, the Upper Austrian to the core, is the person from Traunviertel, and he feels himself as such, too.

The historical roots of the province are to be sought in this district. For historians the Hallstatt culture is one of the most important sources for the centuries before the birth of Christ.

The first findings were made in 1846 by Johann Georg Ramsauer, a mining superintendent. He wrote in his report: "The author chanced to discover a burial field, as yet unknown, by having an area of four square metres dug up with every care in his presence and thus being fortunate enough to find seven skeletons with some items of jewellery and, due to the arrangement of these skeletons, all in much the same position, their heads facing towards the rising sun, the body outstretched, the hands laid alongside the body or across the breast, he was able to recognize a regular burial place."

Subsequently some two thousand graves were exposed and numerous superb burial objects made it possible to acquire a comprehensive picture of that early settlement. Whilst the culture was Illyrian during the Hallstatt period, Celts migrated to the Salzkammergut in around 400 B. C. and during subsequent centuries the entire area as far as the Danube came under Roman rule.

The Romans set up the castellum Lauriacum (Enns) and Lentia (Linz), making Ovilava (now Wels) the capital of their province of Noricum.

After the period of tribal migration the area started to be colonized and Christianized from Bavaria. Monasteries were founded, the Benedictine monastery at Mondsee being one of the first (748) and this being followed in 777 by Kremsmünster and later by many others, like Garsten, Schlierbach and St. Florian which was rebuilt in the seventeenth and eighteenth century. Spread over the entire land, these monasteries and abbeys were the intellectual and cultural, religious and social centres. They provided a decisive impetus, they formed tastes, they were partly responsible for good and bad developments, their traces were deeply engraved in the daily life of the people of that age.

". . . he now presumes to venture a humble

request for gracious recommendation for the supreme appointment of being admitted to the court chapel as court organist or as supplementary deputy master of the court music without stipend. In the latter case the title and the auspicious hopes for the future would be sufficient to secure him the necessary income. He is moreover employable as a clerk and an elementary school teacher, having served fourteen years as a teacher . . . Your humble undersigned servant was born in 1824 in Ansfelden in the province of Upper Austria, having been teacher and abbey organist at St. Florian until 1855, since which time he has been employed as cathedral organist at Linz." The florid obsequiousness, the reverential devotion, the hierarchy, the distressing, ornamental forms of subservience are all rooted in the monastic way of life and thought. At the same time — and it must be seen in context — it enabled the villager, the countrified son of a small cobbler from Ansfelden to become the great Anton Bruckner.

What Bruckner possessed, apart from talent, was human sincerity, modesty, a religiosity which put priests to shame and a naively simple rusticity, all qualities predestining him to become a provincial great. He was a man to whom even Vienna seemed exotic, the fact that, without ever denying his origins, he was able to compose music with a validity irrespective of time and place is an indication of the high standard of his cultural environment. We are accustomed to regarding culture in terms of power, privilege and property. But, just as the wealth of nations does not come from the efficiency of a few, but is the product of work by many, so culture constitutes an intellectual gross national product and it can be traced in all its fine ramifications in every sphere of society. Geniuses do not make a race gifted, a race has to be gifted to bring forth a genius.

The people of the Hausruckviertel enjoy a reputation for being canny sticklers for detail, people who give the appearance of being harmless and reserved, but who come out of their shell at the right moment.

A glance at history provides the explanation. The Hausruckviertel was that area where certain contrasts were particularly glaring. On the one hand the masters, the great landowners, the counts and the sheriffs, ruthlessly pursuing their own interests, and on the other hand the people, the great majority of them serfs, poor, without rights. A fertile medium for the rebellious ideas of the Reformation.

Small wonder then that the Hausruckviertel was the starting point for the sixteenth century peasant wars. From the very beginning the issue was not so much the new Lutheran religion as the desperate attempt to attain a more just social order. An attempt that was doomed to failure, bearing in mind the bands

Hallstatt, copper engraving by Matthäus Merian, Topographia Austriae 1649.

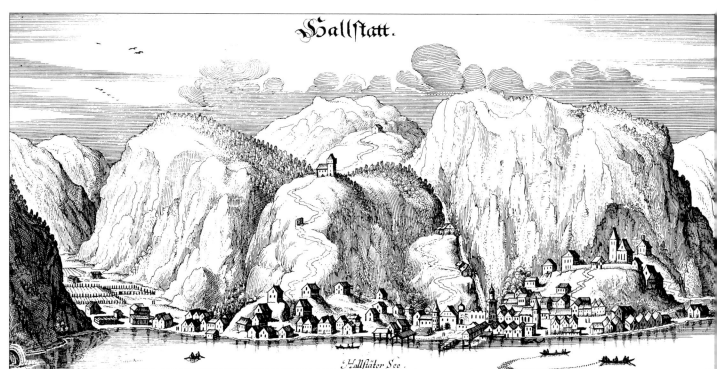

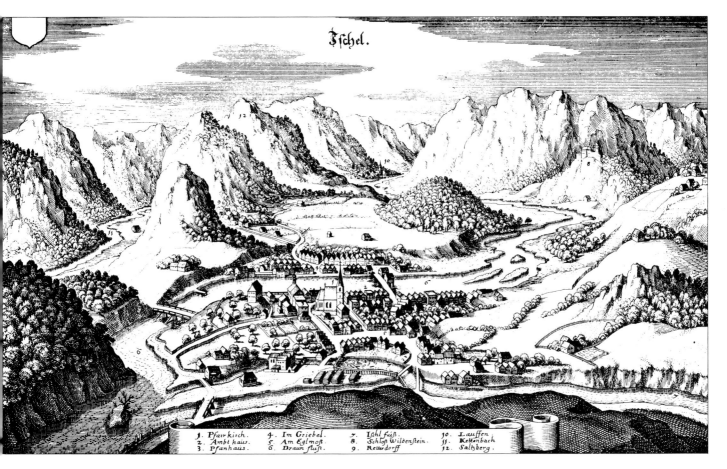

Ischel.

1. Pfarrkirch.   4. Im Griebel.   7. Ischl fuß.   10. Lauffen.
2. Ambt haus.   5. Am Eglmoß.   8. Schloß Wildenstein.   11. Kettenbach.
3. Pfanhaus.   6. Draun fluß.   9. Retterdorff.   12. Saltzberg.

of toilworn peasants, frequently with scythes, flails and hoes as their only weapons, opposing the feudal lords' heavily-armed soldiers. An uprising, however, that was fought all the more desperately and all the more fiercely because it involved people who, in fact, had nothing more to lose.

Only a couple of decades ago every inn parlour in the area contained a painting — it can still be seen today in many inns — showing the "game of dice at Frankenburg". After the peasants' defeat Count Herbersdorf with "his entire retinue of fifty horsemen and one thousand and two hundred musketeers" rounded up the defeated men, "more than, five thousand in number" in front of the linden tree on the Haushamerfeld. He told them why they had all forfeited their lives, but explained that he would graciously spare one half of them by allowing them to throw dice, two at a time. He who lost should hang. So a black cape was spread out on the ground and the men played their desperate game. Seventeen men literally "lost" their lives in this way and were bound and hanged at Frankenburg, Vöcklamarkt and Neukirchen, "being taken down from the noose on the following Saturday".

One of the most bitter scenes in the history of the region and, regarded from every angle, a scene of defeat. It is characteristic that the people of the Hausruckviertel have chosen this scene to depict themselves. The boastful, the heroic would not suit them. They even refer to their home in the diminutive — the "Landl", the little country.

The Innviertel people are slightly more boastful.

> Speaking out and singing loud,
> driving fast and drinking heavily,
> loving faithfully and struggling
> fiercely —
> that's what the Innviertel folk like!

The youngest area of the province did not become a part of Austria until 1779, after the Peace of Teschen. Vienna had hoped to acquire more territory in the west with this treaty and, after a visit to the Innviertel, Josef II wrote to Maria Theresa, his mother, "It is but small, when one considers what might have been, but, in fact, this district is fine and pretty, most convenient for Upper Austria."

Prior to 1779 Upper Austria was divided up into the Traunviertel, the Hausruckviertel and an upper and a lower Mühlviertel. The separa-

Bad Ischl, copper engraving by Matthäus Merian, Topographia Austriae 1649.

tion from Bavaria did not come so easily to the inhabitants of Braunau, Schärding and Ried. The new neighbours constituted no problem, numerous relationships and inter-relationships already existed, but the Innviertel people found it somewhat difficult to accustom themselves to Viennese centralism and Austrian bureaucracy. The Bavarian way was to settle things oneself as far as possible, at table, with a handshake or with one's fists if necessary. And it was often necessary!

The Innviertel people had a terrible reputation for brawling. Looking at the horsewhips, rods, knuckledusters and bullets, lovingly studded with razor blades and hobnails, to be found in rich array in the local houses, and calling to mind the battles . . . the skulls that withstood all that must have been tough!

"Struggling fiercely . . ." runs the song and, according to reliable accounts, the Innviertel people were frequently enough the ones who started the struggle.

The days when bands of youthful brawlers roamed the villages are past, but something of the boisterous wilfulness still remains. "I" and "mine" are the pronouns heard most frequently and "my land", "my air" or "my snow" are said without any ulterior motive.

Those who present such a thick skin to the outside world are frequently highly sensitive and full of humour. The Innviertel people inhabit fertile land, they are accustomed to working hard and harvesting well and they celebrate just as thoroughly. The holidays, the marriages, the funerals, the jubilees and the tributes to worthy men and women are events celebrated in the old style, the population taking a genuine part.

In this area there has never been any real drift to the towns. If at all possible, the Innviertler remains in his traditional place, despite his eccentric bent, he seeks companionship and neighbourliness, sometimes if only to involve himself in dogged, protracted, stubborn feuds about trivialities.

The text will not try to efface what the pictures show: Upper Austria is no place for short attributes. It is not self-explanatory from its history. There is too much and it is too diverse.

Upper Austria is not the Salzkammergut, not Linz, not little Bavaria, not Bruckner and not Stifter, it is not the VOEST and it is not cabbage and smoked bacon. A man from Schärding, taken captive by the Americans in the Second World War, was summoned before a commanding officer. Taken to task by the latter, he was asked if he realized to whom he was speaking and who he thought he was.

The man from Schärding replied, "I'm an Innviertel man and I don't give a damn who you are!"

Whether this incident is true or not, it comes right to the point — the people's self-assurance and their regional pride. The people above the Enns regard themselves in second place as Upper Austrians and in third place as Austrians, they emphasize the excellent relationships with all their neighbours, primarily, however, they are Mühlviertel people, Linz people, Steyr people, Eferding people or Mondsee people, and if it is obvious that these lines were written by an Innviertel man . . . well, why not!

Friedrich Ch. Zauner

Upper Austria comprises 11,980 km² of which 6,765 km² is a permanent settlement area with approximately 1,333,000 inhabitants. Of these some 203,000 live in Linz, the provincial capital, and some 19,000 in the rural district.

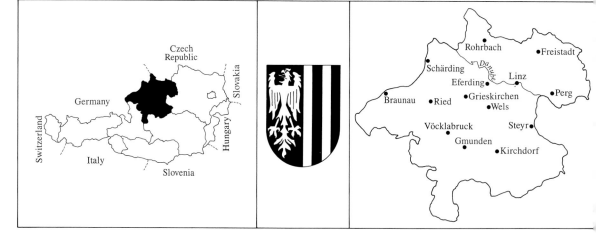

Carinthia

Writing a text to a photographic work is not so much a question of literary talent or, at the least, a certain stylistic fluency. These are what one naturally expects from such an author, if he has a proper command of his role as master of ceremonies for a gallery of enchanting photographic portraits. It is far more a question of social and political values. This applies to all such exercises with the questionable purpose of emphasizing the advantages of a landscape with relish and omitting unpleasant truths with a shrug. It is particularly applicable to Carinthia, however. Like any other patriotic soul who only desires to relate what is best of his homeland, I hesitated for years before attempting such a description of Carinthia; I even hesitated in this particular case where the description is but a pretext for contemplating a series of photographs depicting the sunny side of this Central European island in the sun with as much precise detail as possible. There were very natural reasons for my hesitation, however: that I, too, might not be able to express at least some of the most important aspects of what I regard to be the truth about Carinthia.

For me Carinthia is above all a land of peasant rebellions, a land of proud or merely unassuming opposition by a voluntarily silenced majority in the face of the machiavellian doings of a ruling minority, always acting from the outside, always seizing all the key positions by cunning, force, baseness and pious encouragement. Throughout the entire German-speaking area there is hardly any other region which can have witnessed so many peasant rebellions, such obstinate resistance to clerical and curial diplomacy, aristocratic arrogance and civic lethargy, or, too, such adherence to ancient traditions and cult notions. For several decades now expectant eyes have been directed towards the supposed or real conflict surrounding the so-called minority question. At best this always was, and still is, merely a subject for a few ambitious figures. For the great majority of Carinthians this conflict does not in reality exist, because the character of the Carinthian — whose blood is neither purely German in the one case nor purely Slav in the Slovene case — does not seem to be fashioned for such conflicts. Whilst in Vienna and in Ljubljana this situation is described in the tarnished vocabulary of present-day politics and whilst the few figures in the land itself vie with one another in their patriotic pathos and vain showmanship, the fact is being overlooked that, whether of German, Slav or Romanic blood, the Carinthian has never throughout his entire history accepted any master but himself. In the face of religious and ideological opinions forced upon him from outside he has always displayed that gentle resistance which is not noisy, but self-assured, not dramatic, but in the long run successful. Some of the last vestiges of Celtic cults still to be encountered in Europe survive in Carinthian traditions, insufficiently disguised by Christian ceremonial; in political matters, too, peasant pride was still effective here when elsewhere the peasant estate had long since vegetated into a condition where rights and happiness were lacking, a fatalistic state; peasant anger at social injustice was still flaring up here when nowhere, in those wretched villages with their huddles of country proletariate, could even a thought still be spared for self-determination and independence; Carinthia's Protestants withstood the Counter-Reformation most successfully; Carinthia's first social democrats and German nationalists formed communities with genuinely shared ideals long before the amorphous structures and habits of Viennese party politics; and how stubborn and proud the Carinthian can be is shown by the history of Klagenfurt's becoming provincial capital. Thus it was but logical that after the collapse of the Habsburg monarchy not the Tyrolean, not the Styrian, not the Lower Austrian, but the Carinthian should oppose the threatening loss of ancient homeland.

Nevertheless the unvarnished truth about this country, lying between the Tauern and the Karawanken like a huge trough, seems fanciful. All literature on the subject and what is obtainable by word of mouth, all political and cultural opinions always adopt the same kindly sentimental tone which resounds through the most popular Carinthian folk songs. And to recall my own astonished, impressed or confused glances, my way for decades now of viewing the nature of this land, my way of delighting in the bitter sweet sensuousness of its colours and precisely accentuated contours, signalizes the familiar old view of paradise with minor, hardly noticeable imperfections, communicates the impression of an idyll, the praises of which are unwaveringly sung by a thousand voices and in the most cultured folkloristic manner.

What actually is Carinthia? A palimpsest like every other culture, ruled by many layers of contradiction and adjuration? A misunderstanding to the respective contemporaries who succumb to the error of having merely to hold transient political power in order to have power, too, over the soul of man? An Alpine panorama of colours at their best, fiery sunrises and the winter storms passionately running their hands through the dark green hair of the forest which covers the land like a second shaggy skin? Or is Carinthia merely the unresolved outcome of a historic development which started with the usual confusion of

Hochosterwitz Fortress, copper engraving by Matthäus Merian, Topographia Austriae 1649.

peoples and opinions, solved more or less satisfactorily elsewhere, whilst here the dregs of ineradicable superstition and a remarkable national obstinacy remained? Does the Homerically gifted tongue of those storytellers who attempt to portray the changing fate of the land in variations ever new sometimes cause a dissonance in the thoughts of those listening; is it a speech defect which occasionally makes but shrill noise of much relating to the two peoples settling on the banks north and south of the Drava? Or is the truth that, as a political concept and a moral instrument, Carinthia suffers from the permanently romantic seeming good nature of its people who always know for themselves what to do and what not to do, but who succumb, as paralysed, to any influence from the outside? There is some tragicomic evidence for this last assumption which would be the greatest contradiction in this land so rife in contradiction; for, in mental origins and moral outlook a straightforward peasant character, the Carinthian has always managed quite well to hold his own in the face of foolish authority and irksome alien elements.

But there are, of course, sources which one hesitates to use, less the tale become too rough, too ruthless. There are historic facts which give the lie to the traditional idea of Carinthia as "an island of peace". There is a story in this land which reveals how since the end of the Middle Ages a recurring feature of this would-be paradise was peasant revolt, raging, desperate and, finally, hopeless. Names like Peter Wunderlich, Christoph Groß, Georg Mur, incidents like that pitiful peasant sacrifice in the summer of 1478 when four hundred inadequately armed country people had to confront the invading Turks because the nobility were idly entrenched in their castles and the cowardly citizens behind their city walls, remarks like that made by one Edmund Aelschker who noted with satisfaction some hundred years ago that after the departure of the Turks in the autumn of 1478 the task could at last be undertaken of rendering harmless the peasant leaders by imprisonment and execution . . . all that — merely a random list, dictated by anger — is insufficiently contained or completely lacking in the touched up picture one has of Carinthia.

What is grotesquely remarkable is the truth of the statement that this land never really had to

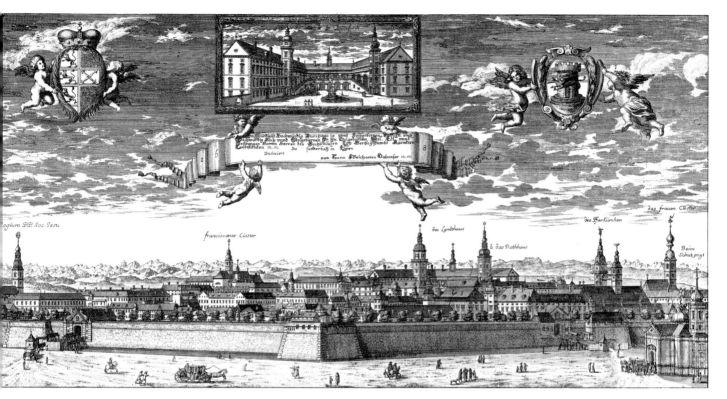

Klagenfurt, copper
engraving by A. Trost,
Valvasor 1688.

suffer a war. And that touching melancholy, that tragic darkness of spirit, expressed for generations in the songs of this people, has with seeming conviction been explained away by Slav blood, Slav mentality, said to be responsible for all that is sombre and dreaming in the Carinthian nature. What rubbish! As if even after centuries the people could free their subconscious from experience acquired, or rather endured, in their dealings with the mighty; as if people's spirits can be divided at will into a Slav and a German half, a Slav and a German sensitivity. Not only is the human individual indivisible, so are his feelings, so is his soul.

There can for instance be hardly any other European region whose present capital city came into being in that one of the peasant revolts — these without exception bore the stigma of social rebellion — could only be suppressed with difficulty by a superior power; and that complications thus arose. The story I refer to here took place at the beginning of the sixteenth century. In Carniola, in southern Styria, in southern Carinthia, peasant unrest had broken out once more, its cause, as always, the exploitation of the country people by the aristocracy and the clergy. On 1st June 1515 more than three thousand enraged peasants met in a little village called Pustritz, not far from the market community of Griffen, where they founded a league, a sort of peasant guard against the despotism of the ruling class. Christoph Groß and Georg Mur, two Lower Carinthian peasants, were elected the military leaders.

The movement quickly spread, taking in Upper Carinthia, seeming to be successful both from a military and an ideological viewpoint, until that moment when the Carinthian estates and the Carinthian nobility, supported by a company of experienced imperial mercenaries, formed up for the counter-attack. Little by little all the peasant strongholds were recaptured; St. Veit, at that time the capital of Carinthia, hesitated to admit the so-called order troops — in fact these were wild slaughterers of peasants — into the city. The reason was not exaggerated sympathy for the pitiful creatures being slaughtered in dozens out in the country, but the citizens' fear of forfeiting some of their privileges. The nobility, supported by the clergy, regarded this attitude as a political crime. The Emperor was appealed to, that somewhat unfortunate Maximilian in his not particularly convincing guise of "Last Knight"; now he was being bothered with the urgent plea that insubordinate, headstrong St. Veit be replaced as capital and princely fortress by Klagenfurt, at that time a settlement of minor importance which had just been destroyed by a devastating fire.

Maximilian bowed to this demand. That was in 1518. The citizens of Klagenfurt feared the loss of their liberties, however, and a delegation was promptly dispatched to Maximilian in Wels to revoke this promotion. But before the Klagenfurt citizens' humble plea could be dealt with Maximilian died; and Klagenfurt remained the capital. The fate of the peasants whose rebellion had been suppressed so ruthlessly no longer seemed worthy even of mention by this time.

And yet this race is famous for its sensitivity, its artistic gifts, capable of lending to the most delicate feelings a clarity and warmth which can compare with any throughout Western civilization. And yet the character of the Carinthian is yielding and supple, he is one of those almost over-sensitive characters who suffer most from homesickness and estrangement and who rise up most passionately against the destruction of their environment. It sounds hackneyed, but anyone wishing to penetrate the depths of these people must look at their lips, must provide an attentive audience for their songs, admiring their musicality. It is only out of this situation, this seamless juxtaposition of self-assured obstinacy and deeply rooted patriotism — no mere phrase in a region like this, where love of one's homeland is almost a substitute for religion — that a unity as demonstrated in Carinthia results; this harmony of the seemingly irreconcilable or the opposing is the secret which gives the Carinthian his tenacity and his enviably light-hearted attitude to life. Although the question remains ever open whether this apparent or actual light-heartedness is but a camouflage: in certain areas of Carinthia there have always been a great number of illegitimate births; as the other side of the picture shows, these are almost outstripped by the constantly increasing suicide rate.

But the historical and socially revealing tales and anecdotes are just as impossible to capture in colour photography as is the social wretchedness of the daily labourers, cottagers, and small peasants right up to the threshold of the twentieth century, or the unbroken self-confidence of the first social democrats who established themselves in Carinthia at the end of the nineteenth century with the completion of the so-called southern railway line via Maribor and Tarvis, or the undeniable fact that this land, said to be so enlightened and liberal,

should until the second half of the nineteenth century have been ruled intellectually and at least emotionally by a clergy displaying certain Jesuitical traits and casting a devoted eye beyond the borders of the province to the fixed points of religious policies.

And yet those lovely colour photographs do not lie when they depict an idyllic, sometimes even somnambulistic Carinthia, a stretch of land which might have been requisitioned by a god of light and glowing colours. In the sometimes barbarically built up areas below the Tauern, the Nock mountains and the Karawanken both can still be recognized, the dark breath of history, in Carinthia usually a little-regarded history of suppression and a lack of rights, and the blazing sensuousness of a scenic beauty which has nothing coarse or vulgar, despite its undeniably peasant character. And anyone with a particularly fine sense of justice need only visit the old cemeteries and look around a little to see how they all — the gentry and the peasants, the chaplains and the labourers, the Slovenes and the Friulians, the Germans and even the flotsam, stranded in Carinthia by many a distant war, the haves and the have-nots, the Social Democrats, the Pan-Germanists and the Christian Socialists — dream together of their resurrection in peaceful harmony. For it almost seems that here opposites only serve to be picked up and then to be made meaningless after a certain period has elapsed.

For a thousand years and more the Carinthian has passionately struggled against any wrong, any form of oppression; the pious murmurings from the churches, the legendary four-part songs, the mighty men's choirs were often merely a disguise for the discriminated small folk's bitter resentment of the privileged great. But with the advent of death, that great equalizer, all anger was forgotten. The Carinthian does not lust for revenge. His sympathetic heart, his sentimental tendency to discover something of himself in the eye of a potential opponent, his mythical passions which have much to do with incomprehensible Nature, signifying temptation and unquenchable desire, all make him an outsider amongst the German tribes and, if he is a Slovene, somewhat of an outsider within the Slav ethnic community. Carinthia is a continent between peoples. And, even if they are newcomers blown here by chance, the people who live

The ice age left some two hundred lakes in Carinthia, the deepest of which is the Millstätter See (141 m.).

a) The parish church of
Maria Wörth on the Wör-
ther See.
b) As at the turn of the
century, the resorts
around the lake provide
welcome summer recrea-
tion. The Schlosshotel in
Velden.
c) Evening in the Wör-
ther See yacht harbour.

a) Rebuilt at the end of the 16th cent., Hochosterwitz is regarded as one of Austria's loveliest castles. The ascent is protected by 14 gates, designed as a bulwark in the face of the Turks, but never seriously put to the test.

b) Roman relief stones, frequently from Virunum, were set into church buildings as from the Middle Ages: Roman chariot on a wall of Maria Saal Pilgrimage Church.

c) The origins of the Pilgrimage Church of Maria Saal, the oldest church in Carinthia, date back to pre-Carolingian days. The present late Gothic building mainly dates from the first half of the 15th century.

a) Erected in 1590, this dragon on the Neuer Platz in Klagenfurt is a reminder of the legend surrounding the town's foundation.

b) Late summer dahlias in the "Europapark" on the outskirts of Klagenfurt.

c) The late 16th century "Landhaus" in Klagenfurt (centre) was erected at the site of the old moated castle.

c

Carinthia harbours some of Austria's most outstanding Romanesque buildings:
a) Crypt of a hundred columns in Gurk Cathedral Church.
b, c) South door and apse of the Collegiate Church of St. Paul im Lavanttal.
d) Cloisters of the former Collegiate Church in Millstatt.

b

c

d

137

The parish churches of the Gailtal contain various precious examples of Gothic and late Gothic art, the most famous being the winged altarpiece in Maria Gail by the Friesach workshop.

Page 139:
a) November in the upper Gailtal.
b) The Roman road above the "Napoleonwiese" at Villach.
c) Evening sunshine on the Dobratsch, also known as the Villacher Alpe.

a

b

c

Famous for its late Gothic altar, the Parish Church of St. Vincent in Heiligenblut has for centuries been the goal of countless pilgrims. They still come here annually across the Hohe Tauern from Salzburg. In the background, left, the Großglockner (3,798 m.), the highest peak in the Austrian Alps.

here have a strange character all of their own, and one never knows whether temperament might not be a better world than character.

The mention of an Illyrian-Celtic, Roman, Slav and Bavarian past is, of course, obligatory in an essay containing all the familiar platitudes about this land; but when one stands on the summit of a Carinthian mountain, on the flattened peak of the Magdalensberg perhaps or on the highest of those wooded terraces which drop from the Soboth down to the depths of the Lavant and Drava valleys, like a darkly colourful waterfall, and when one sees the landscape below gliding away, whilst an aquamarine sky with roughened, splintered ribbons of cloud is suspended above like a mighty banner, and finally, in the late autumn, when one sees the wind rising from the depths of this landscape and the first thin veils of mist at the edges of the woods . . . then history and the precise sequence of historical events are not so important. Then, perhaps, all that matters is the knowledge that the cultures have overlapped for many centuries in this trough of land. One example of this — by no means unique or the most spectacular — is that Four-Mountains-Event which takes place annually on the second Friday after Easter, starting from the Magdalensberg, and which comprises Celtic fertility rites, Slav cult elements and reminders of Germanic myths. Another example is the pilgrimage to Gurk cathedral which is a Romanesque edifice whose walls reflect the light of the Mediterranean, whereas the pilgrimage itself was once mainly a Carniolan, that is Slovenian, exercise, its ceremony going back in part to Byzantine and Roman concepts of religion. Other examples also relate to the greatly stratified customs, the myths and legends, some of which effortlessly survived the years and assured their immortality by donning a harmless Christian garb according to necessity and expediency. But one only has to scratch the surface a little to reveal with astonishment some of the most ancient myths.

In re-narration the danger to which one is always exposed from familiar tales consists of

Spittal an der Drau, copper engraving by Matthäus Merian, Topographia Austriae 1649.

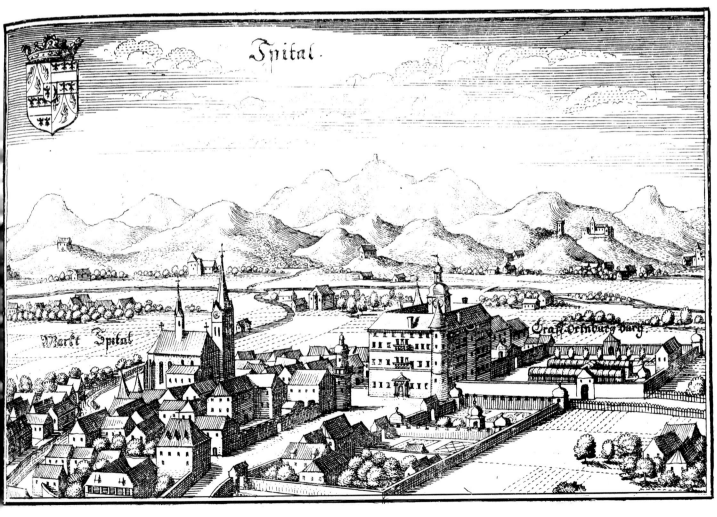

141

the delightful lies which one either imagines or adopts without examination. They have much to do with the presumedly intact state of the scenery, with the poetry of a nature not yet entirely sacrificed to tourism, with the whispering myth of a people who as yet do not contemplate exhibiting their innermost thoughts and feelings to affluent visitors at so-called traditional evenings. It is a fateful chain of lies and irritations, all of which have the same starting point: our half-lost memories of how these requirements which have formed the contemporary portrait of Carinthia came about. The scenery — it exerts such a fascination that superficial intellectual opinion may not only describe Carinthia as the land of folk song, but as the land of painters and poets, too — is only one aspect of many in this connection. The story of the modest or humble Carinthian, as told by historians and writers acting not infrequently on a political errand, is another.

But alongside or rooted as it were beneath all the descriptions of scenery and official versions of history there are still the legends from which everything gladly concealed by history can in certain cases be learnt. I cannot say

whether Carinthia really is a myth comparable with that of Crete where, at a very early time, there was a host of gods and ideologies, a wealth of cultural and civilizing climaxes. All that is mythical in and from Carinthia exists as it were at second hand. As regards ideology, the fact that this is ancient border country played its part, just as the permanent presence of existential fears had a lasting effect. Those Celts and Romans, those Germanic and Slav tribes who settled within the natural borders of this land right up to the seventh century and in parts into the eighth century or who, seen in the light of history, were travelling through on a journey of equal military, economic and cultural importance, those representatives of lost cultures of whose existence there is numerous evidence in the land itself, but who could not really influence our present except in the remains of cults and superstitions, they all merely provide a somewhat exotic background for the actual historical humus formed with the final recovery of the land for Christianity, and thus for western civilization, by the Bavarians who sent out monks and soldiers from Innichen to the south-east. And whatever there might have been of distress and discord,

St. Veit an der Glan, copper engraving by Peter Lessacher and Matthäus Merian, Topographia Austriae 1649.

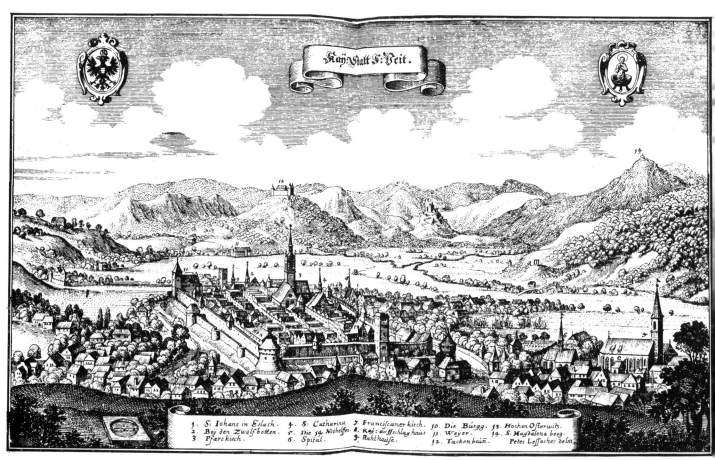

142

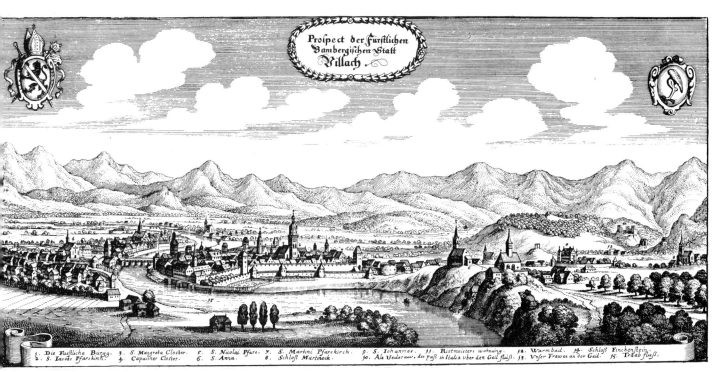

Prospect der Fürstlichen
Bambergischen Statt
Villach.

1. Die Fürstliche Burgg. 3. S. Margreta Closter. 5. S. Nicolai Pfarr. 7. S. Martini Pfarrkirch. 9. S. Iohannae. 11. Ristmaisters wohnung. 12. Warmbad. 14. Schloß Finckenstein.
2. S. Iacobs Pfarrkirch. 4. Capuciner Closter. 6. S. Anna. 8. Schloß Martineck. 10. Ala Uederaw, der paß in Italia vber den Geil fließt. 13. Vnser Frawen an der Geil. 15. Traab fluß.

of privation and creative gesture, of cult and humility, this was now lost in the mists of history, although basically it was only once again a repetition of familiar old requirements.

I am, of course, aware that I am relating these things — they can at any rate be looked up in any decent library — in a very simplified way, as if compressing them with speeding-up apparatus. What on the other hand I find to be missing or insufficiently heeded is the biography of the Carinthian peasants, miners, carters, timber workers and daily labourers, that country proletariat substance who originally still held great political, material and cultural power until this second wave of Christianization began after about the year 1000, gradually becoming a Christianization which worked bureaucratically and covered up any imaginative depths. That delightful image with historical foundations of the Carinthian dukes graciously being presented to the free peasant estate on the Zollfeld, always the political and cultural centre of the land, before taking up their rule — at first their power was restricted — had no positive or educational consequences. This was not altered by the fact that a peasant nobility still existed here, a native aristocracy or élite which emerged from the peasant class and which until the nineteenth and occasionally the twentieth century succeeded in retaining the peasant environment, culture and morals which constitute a major feature of the Carinthian mentality. And

going a step further here to include the latest development, then it may be briefly noted that all social positions in this land originated with the peasant class, apart from a minor small town, petty bourgeois potential. Nor is it mere chance that today practically every Carinthian civil servant, tradesman, industrial worker, intellectual and artist is related to this peasant class and, by way of this relationship if nothing else, hardly runs the risk of not keeping his feet on the ground.

And then, of course, there is that aspect of the matter which at first glance seems obvious — the scenery, that impressive subject for painters, photographers and lyric writers and now above all for the zealous tourist publicity people. There is no serious brochure on Carinthia which does not in words and colours describe the climatic advantages, the idyllic natural beauties, the dreamingly charming loveliness of the "bathing lakes", the gentleness of silent pastures or the whirling snow; over the past twenty years these have effortlessly overtaken all other literary portrayals. Listening to these panegyrics, all of which, of course, have a material objective, one very soon realizes, however, that there is not such a yawning gap between the dream world depicted in the brochures and the reality which is Carinthia. For Carinthia stands up to any comparison with the diction of the tourist trade, usually surpassing the enticed visitor's expectations, mercilessly giving the lie to

Villach, copper engraving by Matthäus Merian, Topographia Austriae 1649.

143

any photographer whose lens does not transform everything to gold, denouncing mediocre lyric talent as dilettantish and altogether giving the effect of a stage upon which only the most striking sets, only the most costly properties have been permitted to set the colourful scene.

For once no mention shall be made of the ravages of time, of the destruction due to environmental influences, of the concreting excesses and the refuse dumps, of the devastated landscape and the building sins which make not only the urban scene, but Nature itself, look shabby.

As a reflective, sensitive and also sceptical person who has found a home here one is always prepared to protect Carinthia from those who praise it most obtrusively and those who slander it most notoriously. But with time one learns that the masterly grace, the inspired architecture of this landscape which outlines the possibilities of life as in stages, the overwhelming profusion of pale blue and dark green contours in a personal union with what I would like to call the Carinthian soul, that all this but serves to confirm in superior fashion any boasting brochure, offsetting any slanderous words, no matter from which bragging mouth, by way of its magnificent normality. Statistical lists are at any rate all that can be offered, parcelled ideas and nebulous figures showing that there are more than two hundred lakes and ponds, hundreds of Alpine pastures, innumerable clear mountain streams, the chalky white outline of towering mountain ranges and the fertile succulence of earthy brown plains; such lists reveal nothing of a Byzantine evening sky in South Carinthia, of the shimmering green softness of a sunrise reminiscent of the North in the Nock area, of the vague melancholy of the Rosental, of the pure simplicity of softly rounded hills in the lowlands, of village idylls and the leisurely pace of life in the small towns, intimations of another bygone age.

Similar is the fate of an attempt at unravelling the lines which give this land its intellectual and cultural mould. The existence or temporary presence of a few reasonably famous minnesingers in once ducal St. Veit and in the old Teutonic Order town of Friesach is frequently cited as evidence of literary traditions. But I regard as more momentous the fact that Carinthia had a socially motivated popular literature long before the obligatory exercises of so-called social revolutionary writers, this even having prompted an aristocrat with the delightfully indigent name of Tschabuschnigg to pose this social question in a nineteenth century novel. Nor is mention ever omitted of the various monasteries founded in Carinthia ever since the dawn of the eleventh century, helping to shape the spiritual and politico-cultural life in the land for subsequent centuries. But the many nameless village communities which achieved a similar effect with far less outlay and with no propagandistic undertone are frequently still denied respectful reverence today.

This very modesty, this almost unique self-sufficiency in politico-cultural matters, too, is typical of the Carinthian. It should not, however, be misunderstood or mistaken for lack of imagination or for mental dullness. A continent like Carinthia is perfectly capable of conceiving of its own all the energy for its continuing development, the material perhaps somewhat less than the idealistic, the party political perhaps somewhat less than the timelessly ideological. Anyone regarding that as something negative should at some time cast more than a glance at the continuum called Carinthia.

Humbert Fink

Carinthia comprises 9,533 km² of which 2,438 km² is a permanent settlement area with approximately 548,000 inhabitants. Of these some 89,000 live in Klagenfurt, the provincial capital, and some 53,000 in the rural district.

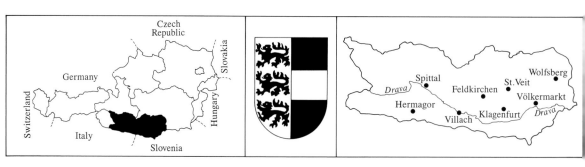

Salzburg

When someone says that he has business to attend to in Salzburg, a house, a love affair, people are generally, although not always, aware that they are unaware of what is meant. For Salzburg is the name of the city and the name of the surrounding countryside, as far as its borders with the Tyrol and Carinthia, with Styria, Upper Austria and Bavaria and, yes, even with Italy at a comparatively tiny spot, of primary importance for shepherds, customs officials and sheep.

The same name duplication plagues Vienna, too, the difference there being that it either poses as a province or a city, depending on what is opportune. Vienna is Vienna, it cannot distinguish itself from itself and if one and the same man appears in the double guise of Provincial Governor and of Mayor, then that is theatricality of the kind that makes Vienna a theatrical city even off-stage. In Salzburg it is understandable that the province has the same name as the city, for it hardly ever meant more than a lucrative environment for the prince in his residence. He alone had powers of decision, spiritual and temporal, the one time and again requiring the support of the other, to such an extent that at times ritual was even abandoned: in 1266, for example, Archbishop Ladislaus was able to enter Salzburg with due ceremony, although he had not been ordained a priest or a bishop, and in 1554 Ernest, Prince of Bavaria, had to forgo the see of archbishop altogether, ten years not being sufficient for him to take higher orders.

Metaphysically orientated spirituality was certainly not the strong point of any of these gentlemen, loving one's neighbour was given the interpretation that everyone was his own neighbour, according to the situation, and the burning of Jews, more than three hundred in number, and the endless procession of banished Protestants bore witness to the love these men showed to their enemies. The pogrom of 1404 in front of the church at Mülln came about when a church thief was apprehended and confessed to having given Jews hosts which they had pierced with nails in order to kill Christ a second time.

On 9th December, 1684 Archbishop Max Gandolf's extradition order was read to the Defereggers. Four days later the first throng left for Augsburg. Children under the age of fifteen were taken away from their Lutheran parents to be educated under Catholic guardianship. As from the turn of the century peace was said to reign throughout the valley, no doubt that same peace left behind by the twenty thousand who had been hit by Archbishop Leopold Anton's emigration order of 31st October, 1731. If it is surmised that the intangible loss caused by this outrage could never be made good, this surmise can neither be proved, nor refuted.

It is certainly not conducive to an understanding of history when the generation alive now measures the past according to its own yardstick, what somewhat unimaginatively is called the spirit of the times should not equate solely with the Ten Commandments and the Gospel, it can only be the spirit of the Devil to kill a man in God's name.

It must be conceded that the Protestant uprising and opposition in 1525 and 1526 and well into Max Gandolf's day was, by way of its social aspect, both religiously and politically actuated. The temporal princes always gave leave of absence to their spiritual part; since, with the exception of Archbishop Friedrich von Walchen in the thirteenth century, they were all foreigners, this would not have troubled them unduly. How fortunate were Rupert (696—718) and Virgil (745—784), those spiritual ancestors of this land: saintlike, they were thus canonized, their sole opposition coming from forests and swamps.

Salzburg, the city, so they say, is beautiful. The province, so they say, is, too. But the city can call Georg Trakl as a witness. He entitled one of his poems "The Beautiful City". There is a difference between saying Salzburg is beautiful and saying Salzburg is said to be a beautiful city. One is beauty perceived, the other is beauty supposed: saying one hears that Salzburg is beautiful. In advertising, word of mouth and rumour become a promise. Brochures have their own truth. As far as Salzburg is concerned, this may be verified from one of the mountains in the city or the near surroundings, from the Mönchsberg, the Kapuzinerberg or the Gaisberg.

Georg Trakl could no longer use that title today. Salzburg, that city of which Alexander von Humboldt said it was one of the three loveliest in the world, seems to be a remnant of history, set amidst and clasped by the Festungsberg, the Mönchsberg and the bank of Salzach. They retain features of the inherited picture. On the other side, at the bottom of the Kapuzinerberg, a good nose is required to scent out the Middle Ages in the Steingasse. Everything else is nineteenth and twentieth century hubris.

Salzburg was abandoned as a fortress in 1861, the ramparts, moats, redoubts and gates being assigned to the city in 1866. With an eye to business, the citizens ensured that the Habsburg dowry was speedily demolished, the traditional becoming the utilizable, presumably a powerful example to that generation of greatgrandchildren in the period after the Second World War. Thanks to concrete and new techniques, they in fact succeeded more emphatically in selling out nature and the past to greed. And, quick to learn, the villagers hurried to present themselves as suburban dwellers, even far away from the city. The heritage was squandered with an open hand, the more so since the citizens' conscience was not at any rate excessively burdened by the responsibility and the ballast of the centuries, their life being confined and cramped in comparison with the pomp and pageantry of the princely court. Their political presence was the same; the fairly decisive attempt to win freedom in part did not make history, but was merely the basis of an anecdote: when the citizenry already fancied itself to enjoy the rights of a free imperial city, thanks to Emperor Frederick III's decree, Archbishop Leonhard von Keutschach, at a banquet to which he had invited the mayor and the councillors, had his guests arrested and taken to Radstadt on open sledges in the company of the executioner. It is said that twelve good men of this deceived gathering at table in Mauterndorf were to be beheaded, but that the Archbishop exercised restraint. In fact, so the story goes, most of them went to their graves prematurely, worn down by fear and the cold of winter. The example sufficed to make the order incontestable for a further three hundred years and more.

Otherwise, too, Salzburg's bourgeoisie were always weak and faint-hearted. The chronicles of opposition to and uprising against foreign rule, against the Bavarians and the French in the Napoleonic era, name villages and little market towns in the mountains, they name peasants and they name miners. Nothing laudable is said of the citizens. Hardly affluent, they produced no culture whatsoever to identify themselves and their estate with works of quality. It is understandable then that the Medicean Wolf Dietrich von Raitenau hardly felt a qualm at having several dozen of these citizens' houses razed to the ground to create space and light for Vincenzo Scamozzi's architectural concept of an ideal city with five squares. After all, it disturbed him little either when the cathedral burnt down on 11th December, 1598. "If it is burning, then let it burn", he is reported to have said on hearing the news. What they should have let burn was the basilica which Konrad III had started to have built in 1181 after Salzburg and its churches were burnt down to the ground by supporters of Frederick Barbarossa during the dispute between the Pope and the Emperor.

When we consider how often settlements and estates were devastated, respect is due to the archaeologists: searching below ground level for foundations — above the surface fire has usually done its work — they secure culture's continuum, where it would otherwise be but the memory of a tale in a story-book in the awareness of many a generation.

Wolf Dietrich von Raitenau was most efficient in demolishing Salzburg. But he also demolished all that was constricted and fusty, perceiving this with senses attuned to memories of Rome. And soon Vincenzo Scamozzi was at hand, Palladio's highly respected pupil. Although Santino Solari completed the work to smaller dimensions a generation later, wherever through the centuries destruction was followed by re-erection, building was carried out in such a way that retrospectively it could be said to have a value and a style of its own, history interpreting the prior destruction as a turning-point. Considered critically, such an assessment rather resembles the retrospective reasoning which finds a purpose in de-

SALZBURG

Salzburg, copper engraving by F. B. Werner and F. J. Probst, c. 1710.

struction — today this process forms part of the armour of those in municipal parlours and assembly rooms who advocate demolition. In fact, however, Raitenau had a total vision of the city in mind when he destroyed. He thus committed his successors from Markus Sittikus to Count Schrattenbach, if we disregard that exception deemed necessary by Johann Ernst when he commissioned Johann Bernhard Fischer von Erlach. Conforming to a tendency spreading from Vienna, the latter and Lukas von Hildebrandt, his rival who was engaged by Archbishop Franz Anton, released Salzburg from its frequently quoted Italianità and the late Austrian baroque style thus came into its own here, too.

Contemplating old views of the city, one wonders whether Wolf Dietrich acted to its benefit or to its detriment, when he cleared away whole parts of the mediaeval town as if it were nothing more than a hindrance. Compared with Konrad III's basilica, Santino Solari's Cathedral is a painful exchange. From the point of view of the city's transformation, its growth and its architectonic variety in the unity of style, one could wish that Wolf Dietrich might have been granted half a century of rule.

Salzburg, the city, does not keep to the middle of Salzburg, the province. To the appraising eye its appearance is most seemly, the Salzach flowing through its midst. Since this river was contained more firmly in its bed in the past century, the right bank has been built up as closely as the left. Here the Kapuzinerberg and there the Mönchsberg lend balance to the view. If one ascends one of these, preferably the Mönchsberg, and surveys the surroundings — to the south they border hard on the mountains, to the east the Gaisberg offers gentle support, to the south-west the Staufen, but northwards they peter out — one might believe all this gives the city breathing space, being the province of the same name which in fact, however, begins fully to unfurl at that point where the gaze imagines it to end, beyond the mountains to the south. For that reason, no doubt, the barrier of rock formed by the Tennen and Hagen mountains was once regarded as an inland border, separating the "Außergebirg", or outside mountains, from the "Innergebirg", or inside mountains. That is handier for the orientation than the customary division of the province into the Flachgau, Tennengau, Pongau, Pinzgau and Lungau, especially since no map informs the walker when he crosses to where, nor elucidates many an illogicality, for instance that the Flachgau, or "flat district", is endowed with mountains, from which it may be surveyed. However geographically uncertain it may be in which district one is enjoying a sandwich or taking refreshment at an inn, certainty is assured by talking to the inhabitants. That, too, is how one learns who or what a Salzburg man is: as such, he does not exist, but as a Flachgau, Tennengau, Pongau, Pinzgau or Lungau man. This seems strange to people accustomed to viewing things and to thinking on a larger scale. But imprecise as the fences and their course might be, the more plainly the people living behind these fences differ from each other.

Unlike the landscape, opening out to the Upper Austrian neighbours in hills and lake hollows, the Flachgau farmer is introspective, far from sociable, not very talkative either, but self-assured. Once he has accepted someone, however, he remains loyal to him in bad times, too.

Although it is only a stone's throw to the Tennengau, the Tennengau man is of a different breed, animated, warm-hearted, quick-witted. With his little farm on the sunny side of the slope and far above the mists of autumn, favoured by the light and spared the shade, he seems to be freed from any competition in the world. Even the cows seem to feel the benefit, peacefully clanking to the pastures to rest, not to gorge as in the Pinzgau.

The people of the Pongau still have the terrors of the Protestant persecution in their blood, its heirs in sensitivity and in memory. Subsequently this area was subjected to the most rigorous missionizing. When permanently endangered, man forms protective mechanisms of orientation. Open enmity would be lethal, dissembling rescues, safeguards from capture. And friendliness is a facial expression. Knowing that helps to explain quite a lot. For the unaware a schnapps occasionally does the same, it is a traditional means of communication here.

Of the Pinzgau man it is said that he is characterized by powerful self-assurance, like the Tyrolean whose neighbour he is. Occasionally his words prove to be louder than his actions, but that only spurs him on to achieve more. The labourers on the big farms are made to feel something of this. The "beautiful days" of Franz Innerhofer's novel are the same as those still found here and there on the Pinzgau man's calendar. He just does not always understand this and finds it difficult to recognize his own guilt as such. They are all hospitable and generous, though.

It is only in the Lungau, however, that one ponders on how to address a farmer, so strongly does he let his ancient lineage be felt. Situated throughout at an altitude of over one thousand metres, accessible from the west only via high mountain tracks, from the north and south via passes which only a decade ago were closed for many days of the year on account of avalanches, more easily approachable in the east, but a tedious journey from Styria, this valley can now be crossed quickly by motorway, primarily by those heading for the Adriatic — the Lungau people themselves prefer the passes, they are more beautiful, healthier than the passage through smelly tunnels. For many years this valley was a bleak waste, somewhat neglected by God and time, but perhaps that is why the Lungau people were not winded when others were exhausted by progress. And perhaps that is why the Lungau man has a brooding, almost philosophical temperament and is adroitly expressive in his speech. After all, as a swine gelder he travelled for centuries throughout the lands as far as the Black Sea and brought back his own ideas to the valley between the Tauern and the Nocken, the more so since in his other affairs elsewhere he was always more successful than his counterparts from the "Innergebirg".

Since the archbishops were first and foremost involved with their own affairs, even though these might be called Salzburg, this name stood for personal power and representation

Built in 1656 to 1661, the Residenzbrunnen in Salzburg is one of Austria's most magnificent baroque fountains; its creator is unknown.

Page 150/151:
Reminiscent of a lovingly arranged stage set: the old city of Salzburg with the fortress of Hohensalzburg and the Cathedral, seen from the right bank of the Salzach.

The Gothic chancel of the Franciscan Church (1st half 15th cent.) in Salzburg.

Page 153:
a) A rainy day in the Getreidegasse.
b) The traditional "Jedermann" performance as part of the Salzburg Festival.

152

a

b

a) View of the Wolfgang-
see with St. Gilgen from
the Zwölferhorn, in the
background the Mondsee.
b) The Wolfgangsee from
the Zwölferhorn.
c) Fishing on the Zeller
See.

Pinzgau farmhouse in Rauristal.

Page 157:
In the province of Salzburg, too, high feast days are celebrated in the colourful old way:
a) festive Lungau costume; b) Pinzgau costume; c) these flower-bedecked poles in Muhr are up to ten metres high; d) the Shrovetide figures in Pongau arouse the forces of nature in preparation for spring.

a

b

c

d

157

158

c

d

The Gasteiner Ache waterfall in the middle of Bad Gastein is the landmark of this internationally known spa; its thermal springs have been in use since the Middle Ages.

Page 158/159:
a) The Großglockner Alpine Road soon after being cleared of snow:
b) Mooserboden reservoir, part of the Glockner-Kaprun power station.
c) The site of a provisional fortification in 1077, Hohenwerfen watches over the Salzachtal.
d) The lower Achenfall, one of the three Krimmler waterfalls, Austria's highest falls with a total drop of 380 m.

This makes good sense when we remember how greatly those estates, from which the compact territory emerged as a firm political structure, in fact resembled the scattered property of a wealthy private individual. From the time of the Frankish Bishop Rupert's foundation of St. Peter's monastery on the site of the Roman Iuvavum shortly before AD 700 until practically the threshold of the twelfth century the property of the Church in Salzburg came entirely from endowments, purchases and exchanges. The cross was carried beyond the borders, but never the sword as a means of acquiring land. Since the various properties did not, however, belong to the archbishops under one single legal title — they did not thus exercise full sovereignty, but merely held the rights of a landowner — considerable areas were lost to the mightier Habsburg neighbours as from the fifteenth century. The present provincial borders date back to the nineteenth century, an imperial decree of 1850 conferring on Salzburg the status of an independent crown-land almost half a century after the secularization of its abbey. The series of events which then commenced resembles a case history: on 11th February, 1803 Archbishop Count Hieronymus Colloredo abdicated as ruler of the province; on the fifteenth day of the same month Archduke Ferdinand of Austria, Grand Duke of Tuscany, became master of Salzburg; on 30th October, 1805 the French occupied the city and the province; on 9th April, 1809 Franz I declared war on Napoleon; by the end of that month Bavarian and French troops were already entering the city; on 30th September, 1810 Salzburg passed to Bavaria and on 14th April, 1816 to Austria; the Salzburg "Landtag", or provincial diet, dates back to 1861 . . .

Dates and milestones of a political demotion. Within several decades Salzburg had lost one quarter of its population. The city fire of 1818 destroyed seventy-four houses on the right bank of the Salzach and did considerable damage to Schloß Mirabell. Twenty years later the ruins were still standing. In 1825 Franz Schubert remarked upon the lack of inhabitants, many buildings being empty, others being inhabited by one or, at the most, two to three families. In the squares — these were many and beautiful — grass grew up between the paving stones, so little were they used. Heinrich Reinhold, the landscape painter, was surprised to find in 1818, before the fire, that Salzburg had only attracted visitors more frequently in recent years; his travel report constitutes some of the earliest evidence that, politically in decline, the city was now starting to exist as a subject for the fine arts, as a prospect, a scene. Events and change are not without example, antiquity is traditionally presented as though it were the prototype of an aesthetic phenomenon for European civilization, its purity only impaired by a few battles. However this may be, those painters who discovered Salzburg for the eye and the canvas abstracted and emancipated the vista, as if beauty were a consequence of the fall from power. Ferdinand Oliver's Salzburg lithographies gave the city its supraregional, now exclusively cultural reputation just at the time when its political decline had reached its lowest ebb. Perhaps this was related to the fact that, unlike in the seventeenth century, baroque works were now missing from the picture. The artists seemed committed to a Sunday landscape in which figures dressed in Sunday best recline, survey and saunter, undisturbed by rain, work or inconvenience. Hubert Sattler's painting of the city fire of 1818 is the only reminder that Salzburg is not, after all, paradise before the Fall.

At the beginning of this century Alois Riegl, the art historian, wrote that at times of a total departure from the Italianate in Salzburg any higher creativity stagnated, people then being content to gratify current art needs in the inevitable way without any undue vitality and with no claim to higher monumentality; Salzburg's significance for the history of art was mainly founded on its always having been an open door for Italian tastes . . .

This verdict requires some modification. Salzburg always was an open door for any culture, otherwise culture of a European standard would never have existed here. Salzburg was first and foremost attractive on account of its situation and secondly on account of its scenery. The people of Salzburg featured there as infrequently as in the history of the art that originated in Salzburg. The city was never more than the scene of operations for operators from other zones. This artistic abstention seemed coupled with a certain petulance, the pretences being financial or social according to the circumstances: even the archbishops' festivities were the occasion for a peevish

Hallein, steel engraving by A. F. H. Nanmann, 1770.

interest in the cost and where the building of a festival site was concerned, public opinion called for a school or a hospital. And, countering the foreseeable interruption, to disregard two thousand years and to concentrate solely on Mozart, as if the period prior to 1756 was an advent, his advent, would be an interpretation disowning further history, for the people of Salzburg managed without Mozart for half a century without this weighing on their conscience. Here, mention must be made of Hugo von Hofmannsthal's effusiveness about Central Europe having no lovelier area than the province of Salzburg and its having been predestined for Mozart's birth. Mozart was born here because his mother's time had come. And the Mozarts had moved to Salzburg because, as Swabians, Augsburg people were all the more free to enter the "Hofkapelle" since it shielded itself from Bavaria and from Austria. Wolfgang Amadeus Mozart is rightly regarded as a Salzburgian on paper alone. He never made this city his own; refractory in behaviour and disposition, he was also, with his father's support, unfair towards his employer. Mozart might well have been a child *in* this city, but he was never a child *of* it.

Salzburg is, however, justified in claiming Joseph Mohr and Franz Gruber, the author and the composer of the Christmas carol "Silent Night, Holy Night" as her own. No matter how this might be assessed, being regarded as a folk song or an amateurish hit, that does not affect the breadth or the duration of its impact. Very soon after the day on which it first was sung it became detached from its authors, the carol being familiar, but the composers long forgotten; some effort was thus required to attest its authorship. Had the Royal "Hofkapelle" in Berlin not assumed Michael Haydn to be its composer, having a search undertaken in St. Peter's Abbey archives for the original the carol would probably have been wrongly attributed or remained nameless. In 1895 Franz Magnus Böhme, a collector of popular German songs, described the origins of this Christmas carol:

Sung by children throughout Germany and enjoyed by their parents, this beautiful Christmas carol is not a folk song brought from the Zillertal by emigrants, nor was it composed by Michael Haydn or by Aiblinger, as has hitherto without any foundation been stated. Conclusive research and the testimony of the true composer himself have shown that the text was written by Joseph Mohr, at that time assistant priest in Oberndorf near Salzburg, in 1818. The melody was composed by Franz Gruber, his musical friend, on 24th December, 1818, the latter at that time being teacher and organist in the neighbouring village of Arnsdorf (not far from Laufen near Salzburg). The carol was first sung on Christmas Eve 1818 in Oberndorf church. A guitar accompaniment replaced the organ which had become unserviceable. The author, a tenor, sang the melody and played the guitar; the composer, a bass, sang the second part; after a quick practice a number of singers from the village sang the chorus by ear. The carol was unanimously acclaimed and was later circulated far and wide.

Every summer, when Austria's Federal President is pleased to open the Salzburg Festival, many of the town's citizens commend the event and their part in it — politicians, businessmen, innkeepers. They are pleased that the Festival exists, but they hardly know, or are no longer aware, to whom they should be indebted. If they knew or were they aware, their certainty of possession and their pride would diminish somewhat. For Hugo von Hofmannsthal, Max Reinhardt, Richard Strauss, Alfred Roller and Franz Schalk — all assembled on that arts council which decided as to the programme and the beginning — were not Salzburgians and, as far as we know, none of them considered accommodating the artistic intentions of a Salzburgian in the planning or the execution. Alois Riegl's decription of Salzburg as an open door proved to be correct in this case, too: Salzburg sets the scene upon which those who have entered through the open door act. The theatricality and the scenario of baroque architecture, the variety of arenas open to a variety of dramas, the hope of being able to play the affairs of men, away from the big city and its rational and calculated forms of artistic work, to a world audience which would not disintegrate socially before and on account of such a play: "The city as the scene" was Max Reinhardt's neat formula that made the Festival an incomparable event. The genius of Salzburg incorporated the festive, but not merely the blithely festive, it did not exclude the present, wrote Hofmannsthal, what it did exclude was darkness without hope or elevation, the profoundly commonplace, the utterly mundane . . . with these reflections he linked the idea of a festival across the centuries with Archbishop Markus Sittikus, that great baroque man of festivals.

The idea behind the Salzburg Festival, its ideology, as defined by Hugo von Hofmannsthal and as produced, although not without loss, by Max Reinhardt, had repeatedly been an object of censure and vindication since the first performance of "Jedermann" in front of the Cathedral on 22nd August, 1920, it being questioned in particular whether an idea was necessary or whether ingenuity of programme was sufficient, this having to achieve perfection for its own justification. Even the lesser calculation — relegating ingenuity to the second row and letting perfection suffice as long as the commercial effect measures up and vouches for the profitability of the entire undertaking — has its advocates. This version dominates at present, supported, too, by the multiple use of artistic perfomance by the media, via which it seems multi-purpose orientated. Those granting the subsidies (and the audit office) thus hold all the trumps, genius playing the losing hand.

In 1918 Max Reinhardt resisted a festival hall for guest performances (for the time being), for a travelling audience and for travelling players because that would be a hotel theatre in which art would never feel at home. When the foundation stone for a festival hall was laid in Hellbrunn park, those responsible were careful to dissociate this from the tourist industry, saying that the festival hall was not to be a fairground for revellers, epicureans, idlers, the empty-headed, or snobs . . .

No one today knows where this foundation stone lies.

Salzburg, the city, and Salzburg, the province, are both, like the entire Continent, strained between preserving their appearance and destroying it for utilization. The rising quantum and the required rise in quantum, expansion as the supreme gauge of human activity, first hit, and enduringly hit, forms and formations of aesthetic rank, it being one of the criteria of form in general that the alteration of one feature alters the whole. Beauty in nature and urban form is not merely a kindness to the eye, but the exterior of an organic effective connection and its continual development. Whether sufficient imagination and vigour were available for the cultural projection of the urban middle classes cannot be established conclusively; economically, they were inadequately equipped. Any requirements for great merchant houses in the Hanseatic mould were lacking, business and trade served everyday needs in the same way as Alois Riegl had noted of the arts. And that has remained the same up to the present day and the bourgeoisie have remained the same in their mental pattern: when in 1842 Salzburg finally clebrated Mozart in a monument, in music and in other manifestations, it was also hoped that the gradual onset of a Mozart cult would considerably increase the number of visitors streaming to Salzburg and thus the revenue of its citizens . . .

On a walk, how fascinating it is to notice how Wolf Dietrich literally drove the townspeople into a corner, how captivating, on leaving one of the narrow alleys and entering the Residenzplatz, to sense the space, the freedom and the light. With the fortress and the Cathedral one has a view of the vertical order of baroque style, the architecture not merely acting as a background to inspire stage direction, even the fear of God forgets itself before this might of God in contour and stone. Building as a metaphysical substratum — that is what temples and cathedrals stand for. And that is what Salzburg, the prince-archbishops' city, stands for.

Perhaps, however, one is not searching for that, but is attempting to find out why even the Salzburgian regards it as a privilege to be and not merely to live, in Salzburg. However much one might investigate, the market in the Universitätsplatz at the foot of Fischer von Erlach's Kollegienkirche should be cited as a reason. For here life still retains something of those urban forms which generations ago drew people to the city.

The market is the glacis of urban behaviour, in the manner of the Greek *agora* it is the place where inward suburban life turns outwards, encountering, presenting and talking. The people know each other, they greet and are greeted, they inquire and discover, what they discover only being important because they have discovered it. It is communication itself that counts and carries weight, not its content, which is readily exchangeable. And the Italian influence penetrates this market, too, three brothers bringing vegetables, herbs, edible fungi and fruit every week from Udine or Verona. When these tireless travellers south

are on holiday, the Salzburgians have to meet their current food requirements in the inevitable way — to quote Alois Riegl once again, but in jest — and to be content with sauerkraut, cabbage, potatoes, root vegetables and whatever other local produce is kept in stock during the cold, cheerless season . . .

Of the province there is nothing more to report in this connection, except that, everywhere where it has remained contryside, it is beautiful farming country in a variety of arrangements, the best acquaintance with its features being made by regarding it in those areas to which not even the most enthusiastic publicity men would dream of enticing skiers or sun bathers. Admittedly, it is a difficult task for the mayors of such villages to feature in statistics and expansion figures, but many a future once predicted to be rosy has, in fact, turned out to be green.

In order to ascertain the wealth of the city and the province, in the "Innergebirg", too, one must count back to the days before the fire, that point at which history started to keep missing lists. Although soon taking up a whole book these will be continued; the cathedral architects have bid farewell to the archbishops millenium; with secularization and the citizenry the engineers moved in, for them Salzburg's history is still a quarry today. That is why metaphysical needs wither and historical meaning degenerates.

When writing about Salzburg, city and province, it is more than difficult not to write an elegy.

Rudolf Bay

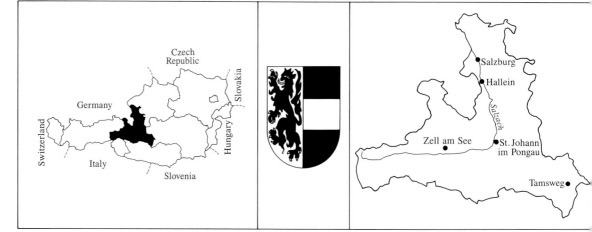

Salzburg comprises 7,154 km² of which 1,555 km² is a permanent settlement area with approximately 482,000 inhabitants. Of these some 144,000 live in Salzburg, the provincial capital, and some 118,000 in the surroundings.

Tyrol

Its name derived from the hereditary seat of the Counts of Tirol near Meran, the Tyrol comprises that section of the central Alpine arc stretching from the northern edge of the mountains to the vicinity of the Berner Klause. This became a political unit in the thirteenth century. Inner Alpine pass country, it is best characterized by its mediaeval name, the "land in the mountains". Politically and geographically, its significance originated in its dominance of the Brenner Pass (1,372 metres) and the Reschen Pass (1,504 metres) the lowest mountain crossings in the Eastern Alps, a connection between Central Europe and the Mediterranean area. Although as from 1363 the area belonged to the House of Habsburg and the Imperial House of Austria, it always retained a considerable degree of independence. During the nineteenth century a distinction came to be established between the German-speaking areas of the North, South and East Tyrol on both sides of the Brenner and the Italian-speaking Trentino, but the unity of the land remained untouched. At the end of the First World War the Treaty of Saint-Germain (1919) truncated this mountain land in the heart of Europe: with the Brenner as the new border, the historic unity was broken and centuries of common history came to a close for the Tyrol. No endeavours on either side of the Brenner can hide the fact that the Austrian and Italian parts of the Tyrol are growing further and further apart.

This anguished history must be borne in mind whenever the Federal Province of Tyrol is considered. Nevertheless, it has retained its own characteristic way of life and it differs in many respects from the other federal provinces of Austria. Due to the loss of the South Tyrol it disintegrated into two sections with no common frontier: the North Tyrol with the river Inn and the provincial capital of Innsbruck and

Schwaz, copper engraving by Matthäus Merian, Topographia Austriae 1649.

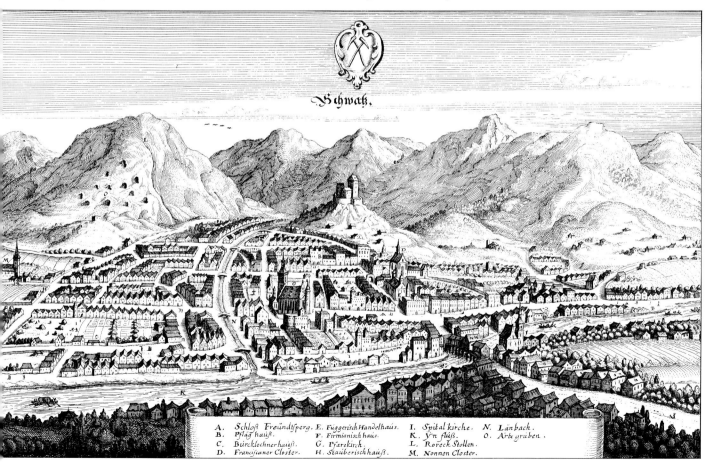

Schwatz.

A. Schloß Freündtsperg.
B. Pflag hauß.
C. Bürcklechnerhauß.
D. Franciscaner Closter.
E. Fuggerisch Handelhauß.
F. Firmianisch hauß.
G. Pfarrkirch.
H. Stauberischhauß.
I. Spital kirche.
K. Yn fluß.
L. Roreck Stollen.
M. Nonnen Closter.
N. Lanbach.
O. Artzgruben.

the East Tyrol in the area of the upper Drau. The structure of the Tyrolean scenery is by no means uniform: the Inn Valley divides the North Tyrol into two distinct geological sections — primary rock in the south and limestone Alps in the north. The valleys in the west of the province are steep and narrow, whilst the Kufstein and Kitzbühel districts more resemble foothills. A similar arrangement can be observed in the East Tyrol where the Lienz Dolomites are part of the southern limestone Alps and the less accessible lateral valleys form a contrast to the Iseltal and the Drautal.

The mentality differs from area to area, too, and in no other European region is there such a variety of temperament, dialect and landscape in such a small space. Despite these frequently very marked local distinctions, the Tyroleans are proud of their patriotic sentiments towards the province; these rise above local rivalry and are only rarely subordinated to feelings of national patriotism.

The Tyrolean displays "the idiosyncrasies of mountain folk to an unusual degree, being to a certain extent phlegmatic, wary and not particularly amenable to innovations of any kind"

Kufstein, copper engraving by Matthäus Merian, Topographia Austriae, 1649.

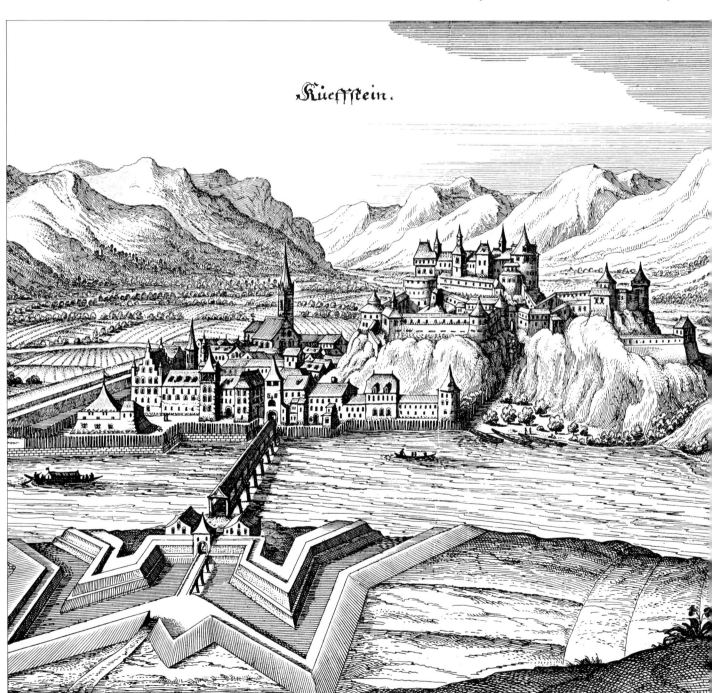

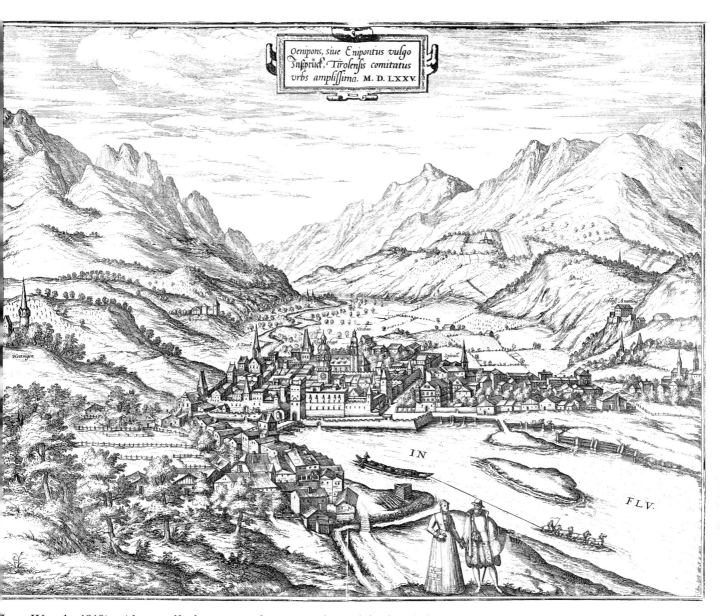

Oenipons, siue Enipontus vulgo Inſprück, Tirolenſis comitatus vrbs ampliſſima. M. D. LXXV.

IN

FLV.

Leo Woerl, 1910). Above all, however, the Tyrolese "show respect for traditional customs of a local or religious nature, which is why any stranger is well advised to approach these characteristics with great deference, otherwise unpleasant consequences can ensue, the character of the country people being somewhat uncouth" (Eduard Amthor, 1874).

Statistics impressively underline that the Tyrol is indeed a "land in the mountains". The total area of the province comprises 12,648 square kilometres. Of this, only 1,603 square kilometres, or thirteen per cent, is permanently inhabited, eighty seven per cent being mountains, impassable terrain and barely cultivated wasteland. The towns and villages in the valleys are usually sited on alluvial cones and plateaux; tiny hamlets, groups of farm-

steads and isolated farms are also found at higher altitudes, but the major part of the province is uninhabitable. "A rough peasant smock, but it warms well", was Emperor Maximilian I's affectionate description of the Tyrol and, indeed, the steep mountain slopes, the inclemencies of the climate and the dangers threatening man and beast have always exerted a strange fascination: the legendary homesickness of the Tyrolean is in reality a yearning for mountains, shelter and protection. Although in the past people here were defenceless in the face of landslides, avalanches and the elements, the Alpine regions have for centuries been put to economic use for mining, pasturage and forestry. The local people soon recognized the strategic value of the mountains as a shelter when warfare threatened and a means of repulsing enemies unfamiliar with

Innsbruck, copper engraving by Georg Hufnagel, 1575.

167

Finstermünz, copper engraving by H. G. Bodenehr, c. 1700.

the terrain. Primarily, the Tyrol has its mountains, as well as its brave soldiers, to thank for the fact that it holds a special place in European history on account of its outstanding defence of its territory; despite modest means, it was relatively easy to occupy the few defiles and to close off the land to the outside. Offering protection and opportunity for concealment and ambush, the mountainous terrain spared the Tyrol from the Thirty Years War and enabled the Tyrolean riflemen to defeat the powerful enemy three times during the Napoleonic wars.

Today, as well as being used agriculturally and as a source of energy (reservoirs, generation of electricity), the Tyrolean mountain world chiefly benefits tourism, sports enthusiasts and leisure seekers. With more than forty million overnight stops, the Tyrol is easily the leader in tourism amongst the Austrian provinces. Within the last three decades one thousand and three hundred cableways and lifts have been built and numerous roads and routes have been constructed. Not infrequently nature has been interfered with in the process and this is the reverse side of an otherwise positive economic development, a development which has brought a certain amount of affluence even to the remotest areas, but which has wrought changes in the specifically Tyrolean landscape, sometimes destroying it irrevocably.

However, there are still many areas which have retained intact their appearance as formed by nature and by man in the course of the centuries and which are now protected by legal specifications. They include many mountain valleys and alpine pastures, like the Ahornboden in the Karwendel, the Mieminger Plateau, Gnadenwald, the Reintaler lakes and the Angerberg, as well as certain areas of characteristic farming countryside, like the Tilliacher Feld in the East Tyrol, the Gurgltal between Imst and Nassereith and the Ehrwald basin.

The Tyrolean landscape and its varied charms can be viewed from the many vantage points and mountain peaks, revealing the beauty of this mountain land, as it was revealed to Professor Max Haushofer in 1903: "The Tyrol! This very name evokes to the eye a magnificent vision of consummate earthly beauty, emerald valleys through which wild mountain torrents rush untamed, ancient towns and tranquil villages resting on meadowy slopes, above the villages, dark forests, white, grey and red rock faces towering up from their shade; above these rocky pinnacles, a shimmering, sparkling awning of ice and eternal snow . . ."

Franz Caramelle

The Tyrol comprises 12,648 km² of which 1,603 km² is a permanent settlement area with approximately 631,000 inhabitants. Of these some 118,000 live in Innsbruck, the provincial capital, and some 141,000 in the rural district.

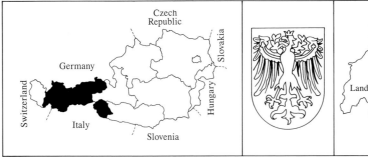

The Riffelsee and, behind, the Wildspitze, the highest peak in the Ötztal Alps (3,772 m.) and in the Tyrol.

Schloß Ambras above Innsbruck is the Tyrol's major Renaissance monument.

Page 171:
a) The late Gothic Golden Roof (late 15th cent.), a symbol of the historic heart of Innsbruck.
b) the view from the Stadtturm conveys the charm of the houses in the old town.

Built for Emperor Maximilian, the tomb in the Court Church is Innsbruck's most outstanding work of art and the most magnificent imperial tomb in the German-speaking area.

Page 172:
Empress Maria Theresa converted the Innsbruck Hofburg into a rococo palace; frescos by Franz Anton Maulpertsch (1775) adorn the Giants' Hall.

173

a) The Winter Olympic
Games of 1964 and 1976
brought Innsbruck
renown as a centre of
sport.
b) Erected in 1765, the
Triumphal Arch forms
the southern conclusion
of the Maria-Theresien-
Straße.
c) View of Innsbruck
from Bergisel; in the
foreground, the basilica
and Wilten Abbey, in the
background the snow-
capped Nordkette.

a) On a November morning: view from Maria Brettfall down to Strass at the entrance to the Zillertal and eastwards to the mist-covered Inn Valley.
b) Thanks to the construction of the Zillertal glacier cableway, the Tuxer Ferner became a demanding, yet convenient skiing area throughout the whole year.
c) Shingled barn in Brandberg with the Grinberg (2,867 m.) in the background.

177

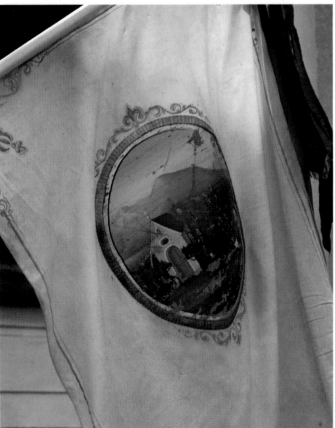

178

In Tyrolean village life festive processions still play an important part.
a) Riflemen at a Corpus Christi procession in Stumm, Zillertal.
b) Flag showing the mounted Corpus Christi procession in Brixental.
c) Riflemen at the Corpus Christi procession in Götzens.
d) St. Isidore procession in Mieming.
e) Girl taking part in the St. Notburga procession in Eben by the Achensee.

e

The medieval route over the Reschen crossed the river Inn at Alt-Finstermünz. This forms the boundary between the "Obere Gericht" and Vinschgau areas.

Page 181:
Superb examples of facade painting are still frequently found on old farmhouses in the Tyrol.
a) Farmhouse with painted oriels in Mutters near Innsbruck.
b) Gasthof Stern in Ötz with Renaissance paintings dating back to 1573 and 1615.
c) Renaissance painting (1576) on the "Platzhaus" in Wenns im Pitztal.

c

d

Chapel set between barns
in the East Tyrol near
Kartitsch.

Page 182/183:
a) Autumn hues on the
Mieminger Plateau.
b) The chalk block of the
Wilder Kaiser in the
Lower Inn Valley.
c) The head of the Köd-
nitz Valley in the East
Tyrol with the southern
flank of the Groß-
glockner.
d) Farmhouses on the
Kalser Glocknerstraße in
the East Tyrol.

Vorarlberg

How does one get to Vorarlberg? Across bridges over the Rhine, on steamers plying Lake Constance, via twenty-three road customs points or through either of the Arlberg tunnels. Both of these are unusually long. The rail tunnel has been in use since 1884, the road tunnel since 1978; they are thus separated by almost one hundred years, a century of unparalleled technical progress. For the people of Vorarlberg these tunnels are symbolic works, the umbilical cord, as it were, that connects them with the neighbouring Tyrol and with the remainder of Austria. Twice a day, the route from Vienna to Vorarlberg is also covered by the silver birds of the "Rheintalflug", but for safety reasons their destination is not Hohenems, the only airfield in Vorarlberg, but Altenrhein, the Swiss airport near the frontier. From there travellers are conveyed to Vorarlberg by bus.

Flying from Vienna to Altenrhein, one might reflect that this one-hour journey is the longest inland flight in our shrunken Austria. Beset by nostalgic reverie or even by historical euphoria, one might evoke those days when a ticket to Lemberg/Lvov, to Czernowitz/Chernovtsy or to Hermannstadt/Sibiu could be purchased at Bregenz station. The train ride took two days. At that time Vorarlberg was situated on the extreme western periphery of the gigantic Habsburg empire, far away from everything. This led Franz Kafka, himself a citizen of Prague, to remark cryptically in 1916, "Bregenz in Vorarlberg — that is a long way".

From the south the province is only accessible across the mountains, over ridges with strange sounding names like Schlappin, Gafier, Garnera or, clearly denoting a border, Fuorcla dal Confin. Of Rhaeto-Romanic origin, this documents Vorarlberg's participation in an early non-Germanic culture. Not until much later was the land Alemannized from the north, where place names such as Eichenberg, Sulzberg or Hirschgunt are of purely German origin. For a long period Vorarlberg was regarded as a mixed zone between the Rhaeto-Romanic south and the German north —

border country. It has remained border country, but in a different way.

Vorarlberg is the Austrian federal province that extends furthest to the west, it is surrounded by three different countries, four fifths of its boundaries — those with Switzerland, Liechtenstein and the Federal Republic of Germany — are Austrian frontiers. The ethnic stock of Vorarlberg differs markedly from the other Austrian provinces, being Alemannic, whereas that of the remainder of Austria is Bavarian. Borders do not restrict, but lend a sense of perspective and Vorarlberg has thus developed an attitude that is both critically pondering and enlightened.

Frontier facts: the heart of the Silvretta is a meeting-point for three regions — the canton of Grisons and the provinces of Tyrol and Vorarlberg. The Naafkopf in the south-west corner of Vorarlberg links three countries — Switzerland, Liechtenstein and Austria. And in the north-west the vast expanse of Lake Constance laps the shores of Switzerland, Germany and Austria. The wide and winding Rhine divides Switzerland and Austria, the canton of St. Gallen and the province of Vorarlberg. To the north, Bavaria is the neighbour. The only inner-Austrian border is that with the Tyrol: the Arlberg. This forms a sharp ethnic and dialectal border and gave the province its name.

Vorarlberg, the land in front of the Arlberg — one might think that the name constitutes a geopolitical subtlety and this is, in fact, the case. Seen from the east, the Tyrol is in front and Vorarlberg beyond the Arlberg. But the name actually came about by way of Habsburg policies. Once, Austria owned a collection of territories in Swabia, Baden and extending to Alsace. These were known as the "Vorlanden". After they were relinquished, Vorarlberg still remained a part of Austria, being directly linked to it by the Arlberg. From then onwards Austria came to an end at the Rhine and Lake Constance; seen from the west, the four domains in front of the Arlberg thus became Vorarlberg.

The fact that Vorarlberg people are of Alemannic stock means just as much to them as their political allegiance to Austria. They are, as it were, dual citizens. That is why their federalistic tendencies and their aversion to all forms of centralism became highly developed and the subject of many a caustic comment. As far as possible, a sort of splendid isolation became the aim and soon after the foundation of the First Republic, by constitution a Federal State, Vorarlberg declared itself to be one of the nine states forming that Federation. Article 1, 2 of the Vorarlberg Provincial Constitution stipulates that "as an independent state, Vorarlberg exercises all sovereign rights not explicitly transferred or to be transferred to the Federation." This attitude of autonomous, political realism has never been retracted.

The province struggled hard and long to achieve full autonomy. It had boasted its own Landtag, or Parliament since 1861, but its freedom of action was still much restricted, the supreme administrative authority remaining in Innsbruck. That era of conditional autonomy was filled with political activity of a kind hardly registered anywhere else in Austria. Long submerged, the Alemannic sense of democracy stirred, inspired by the example of nearby Helvetia. Autonomous ideas thus took shape, spurred on by the Liberals and interspersed with the voices of individual reformers, Franz Michael Felder outstanding amongst them. Others like Jodok Fink, a notable democrat in the old Austria and a brilliant contributor to the foundation of the First Republic, ensured that Vorarlberg's voice was heard in Vienna, too.

Economic and social policies carried more weight here than political issues. Workers' welfare and personal ownership were early concerns. The absence of any proletarian movement at the end of the last century can be put down to such attitudes and circumstances. The building of the Arlberg railway quickly made new markets accessible to the flourishing young textile industry, extensive road projects opened up the main valleys to the mountain populace and electric light was already seen here and there, a symbol of Vorarlberg's pioneering initiative to generate power. Initiated in the dyeing and spinning mills of the late 18th century, textile manufacture became a leading industry, the huge factories being a characteristic feature of the landscape in Dornbirn, Feldkirch and Bludenz.

Embroidery provided a flourishing cottage industry with Lustenau as its centre. In the days of the monarchy Vorarlberg was already regarded as an exemplary industrialized area and today it is still the most industrialized province in the Second Republic. But the potential has shifted from textiles to other manufacturing sectors, first and foremost the electrical industry, metalworking and the production of foodstuffs. The social structure has changed considerably, the great majority of employees working in trade and industry and the farmer standing somewhat apart, an individualist who is secretly envied by many. The rural atmosphere of the province is still upheld in many people's activities, be they gardening, fishing or hunting, and even large industrial companies have their own farmsteads here and there. The Alemannic bond with the soil lives on. Thus the Rhine Valley Walgau industrial zone is characterized by suburbanization; the typical mixed landscape in the areas industrialized at an early date gave rise to a semi-urban scene that causes a headache to regional planners, particularly since eighty per cent of the province's entire population (331,000) live in the area between Bregenz and Bludenz. The fact that the towns, market communes and industrial centres have extensively retained their character is due to the strong Alemannic sense of tradition and to that rather astute way of allowing each his own.

The variety of Vorarlberg's landscape is a source of surprise. Between an expansive lake district and a zone of high mountains is a plateau area that sinks into hilly country in the north-west. The altitude of the province rises from 400 to 3,300 metres within only eighty kilometres, a remarkable gradient for such a small area and one of the reasons for the early rise of tourism. The Bregenzerwald, Kleinwalsertal and Montafon became popular summer destinations thanks to their hospitable villages and an extensive Alpine zone, the demanding routes in the Silvretta and the Rätikon also attracting alpinists. The Tannberg and Arlberg areas only acquired their renown later with the advent of winter sports. Bregenz, the provincial capital, provides a feast for the eyes thanks to its lake and the nearby mountains; in summer it is a magnet for a never-ending stream of tourists. Resting in a wide basin of the Rhine Valley, Dornbirn is

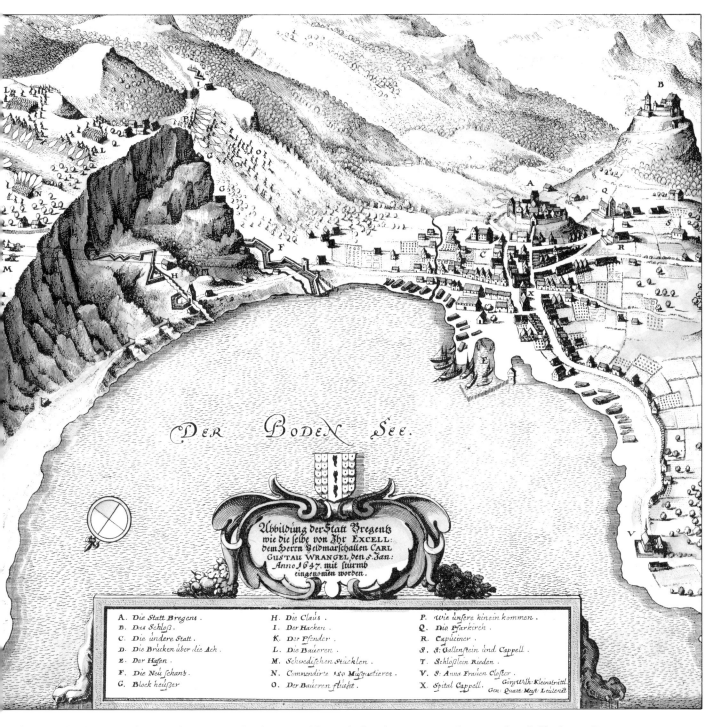

Bregenz, copper engraving by Görg Wilhelm Kleinsträttl and Matthäus Merian, Theatrum Europ. V. 1647.

ndisputedly the most industrious town in the province, its people known for their Alemannic thrift. Hohenems is the youngest of the towns, only having been elevated to this status in 1983. It is proud of its past as an imperial county, of the "Schubertiade" Festival that was conceived within the walls of its palace and of its Jewish Museum, opened in 1991. The motorway winds through the Rhine Valley and on to Bludenz and the Arlberg tunnel. It only requires a good hour to drive through both main valleys in the province, but those taking their time can enjoy to the full the seductive scenery of the Rhine Valley, the Walgau and the Klostertal.

It is indeed a fascinating thought that the Rhine Valley is the biggest north-south furrow in the entire Alpine area; constituting the boundary between the eastern and western Alps, it was formed by the Rhine glacier and its vastness is impressive. Travellers with an interest in archaeology soon strike gold: the Swiss side provides a glimpse of the Palaeolithic, the Vorarlberg side revealing traces of the following Mesolithic and Neolithic stages. The ancient north-south route through the Rhine Valley suddenly takes shape. After the Rhaetians the Romans were the first people to develop the route properly and they established one of Europe's first north-south axes here. The direct line via the Danube, Lake Constance, Chur, Julier, Maloja and Milan was one of the major arterial routes for Rome's armies and merchants, the very first trans-alpine connection. It was at that time that Brigantium, the Bregenz of today, acquired its outstanding role as the main place on Lake Constance and in the surrounding territory. Quickly developing into a Roman city, it first flourished two thousand years ago.

When "Bregenz 2000" was celebrated in 1985, the town experienced a birthday of more than archaeological provenance and a spectacle of a special kind, Jérôme Savary's production of Mozart's The Magic Flute being performed on the lake and bringing new dimensions and deserved recognition to the annual festival.

As befits neighbours, Bregenz and Dornbirn enjoy vying with one other. One claims to be the most beautiful, the other the most industrious. Both are applicable. One is the provincial capital, the other the largest town in the province and, since Bregenz had long boasted a cableway on the Pfänder, Dornbirn built its own such installation on the Karren. From there, in Dornbirn's opinion, the panoramic view is even more magnificent than that from the Pfänder. Bregenz organized its festival, Dornbirn its textiles fair. What culture is for the one, trade is for the other. Bregenz is the site of the Vorarlberg Provincial Museum, Dornbirn houses the Vorarlberg Natural History Exhibition. Dornbirn likes to excel in everything — even its Martinmas market now far surpasses the Bregenz "Klosa" market.

As Europe's biggest freshwater delta, the Vorarlberg lake district is attracting increasing popularity and attention. It extends across part of the banks and part of the waters of Lake Constance between the Alter Rhein and the Fußacher canal. 293 of the 450 European species of birds can be found in the Rhine delta, many of them threatened by extinction. For the time being their survival is assured, however, thanks to the protective measures taken by Vorarlberg as its contribution to conservation. Some 5,000 acres of marshland thus remain a habitat for animals and plants alike.

Since the early days of tourism the panorama from the Pfänder above Bregenz (1,066 metres) has enjoyed renown. The Germans are provided with a view across Lindau, once an imperial city, to the hills of upper Swabia, the geologically interesting morainic scenery of the former Rhine glacier, and down to Constance. The Swiss see their Appenzell-St. Gallen range of mountains from the Säntis to the Pizol and on to the Glarus and Grisons Alps. At night the Swiss mountain villages are linked by a sparkling chain of light and during the Second World War this sight accentuated the contrast with Vorarlberg, everything this side of the Rhine being shrouded in darkness during the blackout. From the Pfänder the people of Liechtenstein can also glimpse a fragment of their principality with the Drei Schwestern (2,035 metres) towering above. Other peaks in this range can be seen to the east and the Brandner glacier can also be made out when visibility is good. The view eastwards is extensive and stretches to the Tyrolean boundary; focal point of the Bregenzerwald mountains, the Kanisfluh rears up in the middle of our field of vision. To the north the lush green of the Algäu is so vivid that one seems to actually hear the cowbells, a scene that might have come from the brush of Grandma Moses.

The vast expanse of Lake Constance gleams below, aptly called the "Swabian Sea". In around A.D. 350 Ammianus Marcellinus, the Graeco-Roman military historian, probably stood here. He provided his readers in faraway Italy with the first account of the Rhine and with a description of how the waters of that river merge with Lake Constance, a natural spectacle to be seen annually on clear spring days, when the dark water of the Rhine leaves its imprint on the turquoise surface of the lake Vorarlberg only has a small share (26 kilometres) in the 263 kilometre circumference of Lake Constance; from the Rhine delta to Bregenz harbour the banks remain flat, rising steeply on the short stretch to Lochau. In the evening, when the sun rolls away in the distance, as if extinguished by the water, the view from the top of the Pfänder is bewitching, reminiscent of a seascape, prompting an awareness that this view extends the furthest westwards of any in Austria.

The Bregenzerwald, the largest valley in the province, is special in many ways. Once magnificent farming land, it reflects the pleasantly

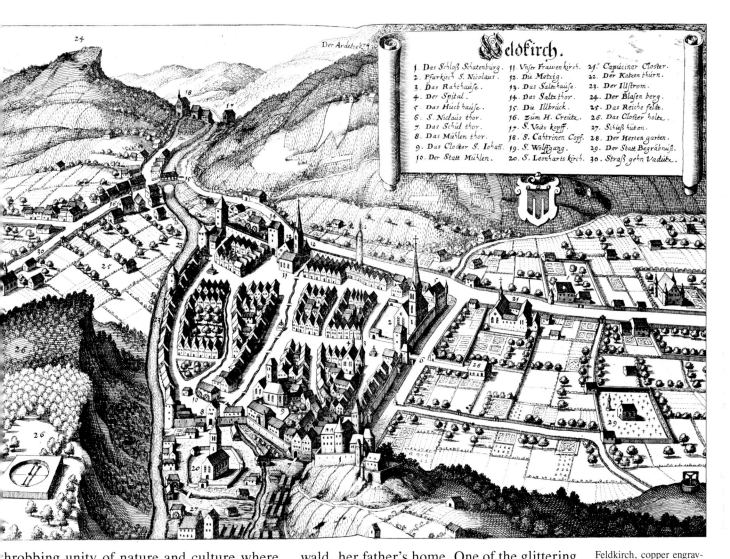

Feldkirch.

1. Das Schloß Schatenburg.	11. Vnser Frawen kirch.
2. Pfarkirch S. Nicolaus.	12. Die Metzig.
3. Das Rahthause.	13. Das Saltzhause.
4. Der Spital.	14. Das Saltz thor.
5. Das Huchhause.	15. Die Illbrück.
6. S. Niclaus thor.	16. zum H. Creütz.
7. Das Schül thor.	17. S. Veits kopff.
8. Das Mühlen thor.	18. S. Cahtrinen Copf.
9. Das Closter S. Iohan.	19. S. Wolffgang.
10. Der Statt Mühlen.	20. S. Leonharts kirch.

21. Capuciner Closter.
22. Der Katzen thürn.
23. Der Illstrom.
24. Der Blasen berg.
25. Das Reiche felde.
26. Das Closter holtz.
27. Schieß hüten.
28. Der Herren garten.
29. Der Statt Begräbnuß.
30. Straß gehn Vadütz.

throbbing unity of nature and culture where man alone — rural man — calls the tune. This is a world of gentle foothills and obviously mountainous terrain. Practically cut off from the rest of the world until the nineteenth century, the area developed a much extolled sociopolitical structure that won respect and envy. It was once a place of unusual freedom, comparable perhaps with the early Swiss cantons, and its autonomy became a tradition that was visible and audible in architecture, language, customs and ideas. During the baroque era, in the seventeenth and eighteenth centuries, the young men thronged to Swabia and Switzerland to work as masons and plasterers, becoming great master builders and architects and creating works of a mainly sacred kind. These went down in general art history under the collective name "Vorarlberg baroque".The men were followed by a successful woman: Angelika Kauffmann (1741—1807). She came from Chur in the Grisons, but felt that she belonged to Schwarzenberg in the Bregenzer-

wald, her father's home. One of the glittering stars in the eighteenth century art firmament, she was a member of the Royal Academy, a friend of Reynolds, of Goethe in Rome, of the Queen in Naples. To manage all that in those days a woman must have possessed outstanding gifts and been a strong personality. Angelika Kauffmann has gone down as such in the history of art.

When the Bregenzerwald comes to an end and the Tannberg shapes the uppermost Lechtal, the scenery alters slightly. Here, jagged rocks tower up above the fields and pastures and one is almost reminded of the Dolomites. In the fourteenth and fifteenth centuries the Tannberg was settled by the Walser, immigrants from the Swiss Valais, Alemannic people with a strange dialect which still colours their descendants' speech today. This movement of Walser folk in search of land went further than the Tannberg, some of them moved down into the upper Breitach valley, establishing a new home there — the Kleinwalsertal. They were

Feldkirch, copper engraving by Matthäus Merian, Topographia Sueviae 1643.

189

strong people and they still form the core of the population. The wide valley only has one opening — to the Algau in the north. High mountain ridges inhibit any access from the Bregenzerwald or the Tannberg and thus, although belonging to Vorarlberg, this valley could always only be reached from Germany or on foot across the mountains. Their isolation from Austria prompted the people of Kleinwalsertal to form a customs union with the kingdom of Bavaria in 1891 and that agreement is still in force; that is why the German mark, and not the Austrian schilling, is still the standard monetary unit there. German customs officials and Austrian police go about their duties in friendly rivalry, the inhabitants display their allegiance to Vorarlberg and to Austria, although their business activities — primarily the flourishing tourist trade — are understandably directed towards Germany. Here, too, tourism destroyed the only Walser scattered settlement almost entirely, so that the three villages of Riezlern, Hirschegg and Mittelberg will probably soon have grown into one large commune.

Once the Tannberg was Vorarlberg's highest farming area with settlements extending up to an altitude of 1,800 metres; two of them, Bürst-

egg and Hochkrumbach, were abandoned at the end of the last century. Since the development of the Flexen road at the beginning of this century and due to a change in the traffic situation the Tannberg became a part of the Arlberg catchment area, particularly after the advent of winter sports. The rural character of the district was destroyed by tourism, but the natural splendour has remained, taking on glittering forms in the winter. Thanks to their vast slopes, devoid of trees and extensively secure from avalanches, Lech and Zürs became an eldorado of skiing, attractive resorts with an international reputation. Skiing's hour came early on the Arlberg, a handful of ladies and gentlemen learning how to glide in the snow on tapering boards in 1906. That was probably one of the very first skiing lessons and the legendary beginning of Alpine skiing.

Divided into a Tyrolean and a Vorarlberg skiing region, as is proper amongst relatives, the Arlberg acquired its world reputation not purely on account of those early beginnings, personified by the legendary Hannes Schneider of Stuben, but also thanks to the development of a style of skiing called the "wedel technique" which made skiing more or less a mass sport.

Bludenz, copper engraving by Matthäus Merian, Topographia Sueviae 1643.

190

ass and mountain at the same time, the Arlberg lays more than a local claim to fame. As continental watershed, it divides the tributaries of the Rhine and the Danube and is frequently a weather divide, too. In inner-Alpine communications the Arlberg route always constituted a point of intersection, it was the salt route between the Inn Valley and the Rhine Valley, a mule track and, thanks to Joseph II, that progressive Habsburg monarch, a skilfully built highway. The dense forest of arolla pine had already been swept away by the destructive might of avalanches in those days and what has since remained is boulders and detritus, the habitual desolation of pass scenery.

In 1363 the Habsburgs acquired the Tyrol; they remained at the ready on the Arlberg in order to advance to the Rhine and Lake Constance. This was the hour of Vorarlberg's birth. Centuries later, in the reign of Francis Joseph I, the Arlberg route assumed a new significance thanks to the construction of the railway. With a length of 10.3 kilometres, the Arlberg tunnel created a sensation in those days and it has gone down in railway history as a feat of engineering. Its brother, the road tunnel opened in 1978, is somewhat longer, a masterly example of the new Austrian tunnelling method.

Running down from the foot of the Arlberg to the Walgau, the Klostertal derived its name from the cloister that was founded in the late Middle Ages to look after the Arlberg route. Later, further accommodation for travellers was provided in the place now known as Stuben and soon afterwards the hospice was erected at the summit of the pass and named after St. Christopher, patron saint of travellers. Founded thanks to the charitable work of one Heinrich Findelkind, it serves as a permanent reminder of the hazards this route once implied.

At the site of the cloister a chapel originally provided a place of worship for the miners who worked the southern slopes of the Klostertal in the early and high Middle Ages, searching for ore and, above all, silver. They were the first settlers in the valley, followed much later by farming folk, road-makers, blacksmiths, ostlers, drovers, carters and, finally, railwaymen. Typical roadside villages thus developed, everyone proffering his trade to wayfarers. Farming never became established in a big way, the valley is too narrow and there was never much room for affluence either. Industry did not penetrate here, but tourism has recently gained a footing, the rocks and wooded slopes, the gorges and waterfalls attracting visitors in search of peace and solitude.

Bludenz boasts a favoured position, a meeting-point for five valleys, a landscape created with a lavish hand. The little town is captivating thanks to its old centre, the medieval arrangement of which cannot be mistaken. A country town, fattened up by the railway and by industry, Bludenz is also the place where in 1873 the German and Austrian Alpine Clubs were fused, remaining the largest such association in the world until 1938, that calamitous year. The letters D.Ö.A.V. on old hut signs and signposts are a reminder of that joint association. Like all of the high valleys in the province, the Montafon was originally only a pasture area, becoming a permanent settlement from nearby Walgau, partly due to the pressure of Roman rule and partly due to migrations caused by the invasion of the Alemanni. The discovery of ore also accelerated settlement. This cultural phase lasted far longer in the Montafon, a sort of Rhaeto-Romanic stronghold, than in the remainder of Vorarlberg where the process of Germanization was quick. Contact with the Walser migrations eventually led to a mingling with Germanism in the Montafon, too, but characteristic Rhaeto-Romanic features remained, one example being the old stone house with a wooden parlour extension — the origin of the Montafon house still greatly admired today. Its exterior decoration is of a later date, however, and can be attributed to the baroque; it was here, if anywhere in Vorarlberg, that the demi-heaven of Austrian peasant baroque found expression.

Forty kilometres long and traversed by the waters of the upper Ill, the main valley is surrounded by three massifs: the Rätikon, Silvretta and Verwall. Only two of the numerous lateral valleys are permanently settled — the Silbertal and the Gargellental. Otherwise narrow, the valley widens out in the Schruns-Tschagguns basin; with its favourable climate, this is one of the most popular areas for rest and recuperation.

Picturesque is an adjective frequently used in connection with the Montafon and, indeed, spruce villages, farmsteads, alpine chalets and great expanses of pasture and moorland are a visual delight in the changing hues of the seasons. The striking sights include the Zimba with the Vandanser Steinwand, the Gauertal — the Drei Türme and the Drusenfluh form its unique culmination — and, further south, those proud peaks, the Litzner-Seehorn, and finally the Große Buin with its huge frame, the highest mountain in the province (3,312 metres).

The Walgau extends from Bludenz down the Illtal to Feldkirch and is one of the oldest settlement areas in the province, as documented by Rhaeto-Romanic strip farming, the clustered village and the central passage arrangement of the houses. Many places still harbour unadulterated examples of the Gothic style, usually in sacred buildings. Once, the Walgau was called the "Welschengau" and formed the backbone of the Rhaeto-Romanic section of the population, joined during the feudal age with the Werdenberger-Sargans line of Montforts whose castles still impress as ruins and the home of legends. The German element did not gain the upper hand until the late Middle Ages, again aided by the Walser migration. The Walser occupied all of the heights on the northern side of the Walgau and the valley of the Lutz, the area known as the Große Walsertal and having the most authentic Walser form of single farmhouse with separate living quarters and cowsheds. Many a home in this district fell victim to avalanches and the destruction of most of the village of Blons in the catastrophic year of 1954 remains a vivid memory. The Walser farmer has nevertheless remained a stalwart example of the will to survive.

To the south of the Walgau the Rätikon massif rears up, furrowed by narrow side valleys of which the Brandnertal alone is permanently settled. From Brand the Rätikon peaks are almost within touching distance — the Zimb[a] and the Schesaplana, two traditional moun[n]taineering favourites. The narrow, woode[d] Gamperdonatal harbours a gem of solitude a[t] the head of the valley, the Tann opening ou[t] unexpectedly into a wide, sunny expans[e] known as the Nenzinger Himmel. The Rätiko[n] falls down abruptly to the Rhine Valley, i[ts] western shoulder a part of Liechtenstein. Fu[r]ther north, where the Ill squeezes a pat[h] through a gorge, Feldkirch can be seen.

For centuries Feldkirch was regarded as th[e] foremost of the four domains in front of th[e] Arlberg. After 1728 it gradually relinquishe[d] this pre-eminence, the prefecture in Bregen[z] having been declared the chief administrativ[e] office. Ever since its medieval beginning[s] however — the Montforts transferred thei[r] main seat from Bregenz to Feldkirch in 1188 -[] Feldkirch was of prime importance. It wa[s] here that the estates first convened in 1541, [it] was here that a school of Latin was establishe[d] in 1418 and a grammar school in 1649. Fel[d]kirch is a centre of education, a centre o[f] humanism, the names it has brought forth hav[e] acquired renown far beyond the confines of th[e] province. Its citizenry nurtured education an[d] the arts and provided fertile ground for specia[l] achievements. In Wolf Huber (c. 1480—1553[)] unmistakably an exponent of the Danub[e] School, it possessed a painter of the first orde[r] and in Georg Joachim Rhetikus (1514—1574[,] pupil of Copernicus, a scientific genius whos[e] uniqueness radiates into our nuclear age.

Feldkirch's ancient buildings have recentl[y] been restored, the valuable late medieva[l] essence thus being preserved for posterit[y] This has reinforced people's awareness tha[t] the meaningfully gauged norm was onc[e] regarded as the only valid criterion of aestheti[c] sensibility.

Walter Lingenhö[l]

Vorarlberg comprises 2,601 km² of which 610 km² is a permanent settlement area with approximately 331,000 inhabitants. Of these some 116,000 live in Bregenz, the provincial capital.

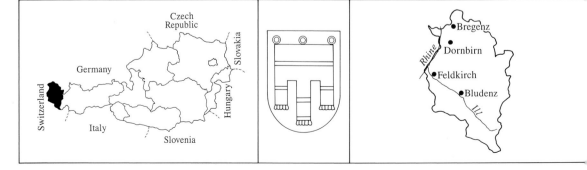

192

Late Gothic frescos adorn the outside wall of the 14th cent. Parish church at Tisis near Feldkirch.

Page 194/195:
a, d) Cherry blossom at Fraxern above the Rhine Valley, home of the popular "Fraxener Kirschwasser".
b) The ancestral seat of the counts of Montfort, the Schattenburg was originally built in the early 13th century and is the most notable castle in Vorarlberg.
c) The Rote Haus in Dornbirn, a characteristic 17th cent. Rhine Valley house, is now a restaurant in the town's pedestrian precinct.

c

d

a) Stage set for
"Nabucco" on the lake,
Bregenz Festival, 1993.
b) Lake Constance is
ideal for sailing.
c) View of Bregenz bay
with the harbour and fes-
tival hall (right, on the
banks of the lake), seen
from Haggen.

196

c

The return of the cattle from the summer pastures in mid-September is a festive occasion in Schwarzenberg in the Bregenzerwald and the welcome is warm in the village centre.

Page 200/201:
View of the wintry Arlberg skiing panorama with St. Christoph, seen from the Valluga. The Arlberg is an annual skiing rendezvous for international celebrities.

a) The Montafon skiing area of Golm above Schruns-Tschagguns also fulfils skiers' every wish. b, c) The water stored in the Silvretta reservoir provides a clean source of energy for Vorarlberg and its neighbours.

The late Gothic parish church of Mittelberg in the Kleinwalsertal (c. 1463).